Lacrosse Goaltending II

Lacrosse Goaltending II

HOW TO COACH AND PLAY LACROSSE GOAL
AND OTHER STORIES ALONG THE WAY

By Jon D. Weston
Itinerant Lacrosse Vagabond and Coach

ISBN: 978-0-9801273-0-0
Published by Weston Lacrosse
Copyright © 1997, 1998, 1999 as Lacrosse Goaltending for Coaches (Players too)
Rewritten and Copyright © 2008 as Lacrosse Goaltending II by Weston Lacrosse
and Jon Weston
1st Edition as Lacrosse Goaltending II

For information address: Jon Weston,
    Weston Lacrosse
    5920 Bethlehem Court
    Rockville, MD 20855
    301-294-3234
    westonlax@aol.com
    www.thegoalieman.com

Publisher:Weston Lacrosse
Cover:RC Communications LLC (www.selfpublishing.com)
Cover Photographs: Ben Legg of Charlie Legg, Bowdoin College and of Jon
Weston, The Goalieman
Printed in the United States of America

Contents

Dedications

Hunky, My Friend This book is dedicated to Arthur Hungerford LaMotte (1936 - 1996), the founder of the Magruder High School Lacrosse program and the finest friend a player or coach could have. His friends and family called him "Hunky".

Hunky, you are missed. I hope that this book is a partial tribute to you and the way that you so graciously treated everyone, especially the young people that you coached or gave me the chance to coach.

Justin & Todd The 1994 season of Magruder High School outlook was bright. With a strong returning attack, good middies and an All-Star defense, Justin McCarthy, a junior, was to take over the reins from all-league goalie, Ian Robertson, who had graduated. With Todd deStwolinski coming in as a freshman as the backup, we looked solid in goal.

On March 1, opening day of practice, Justin McCarthy died in an automobile accident. Justin's death left us without an experienced player in goal and it left me without a key friend. Teaching Todd got to be a priority. I soon realized there was a void in organized and effective teaching tools and techniques for lacrosse goalies.

Thus, this book is dedicated to Justin, in memoriam, and to Todd, in life, so that others can learn/teach easily.

Acknowledgments

Jeff, My Teacher I would most like to thank Jeff Singer for being patient enough to teach me to play goal. His insight and dedication to playing the position well spilled over onto me. He read the earliest drafts of this book and all of his comments have been incorporated. They were excellent.

Karen, My Wife Thanks to Karen Weston, my wife, for her tolerance of my life long diversion; lacrosse, and to the hours of reading, editing, filming, commenting, carrying equipment, clinics and other activities that make this book and my life better.

Goalies Thanks to the many goalies along the way who have helped me and this book including;

Geoff Berlin (Johns Hopkins University '68) – A great JHU goalie and classmate, who became an even better friend since.

Jeff Singer (MIT, '77, Washington Lacrosse Club) - goalie extra-ordinaire for WLC, and a friend / teacher for decades

Rodney Rullman (UVA '76, NCAA Champion) - Vail Masters competitor and friend. His complementary and constructive comments are included in this book.

Dan Mackesey (Cornell '76, 2 time All-American, NCAA Champion, Team USA 1978) - Our Vail Masters team goalie, friend and contributor to this book.

Don West (Baltimore Thunder) - Teammate and friend on local championship indoor and outdoor teams.

Brian Dougherty (Maryland '96, 2 time All-American, Team USA '98) - Brian helped teach goalies at the NCAA Youth Education through Sports (YES) clinics at University of Maryland -- I learned a lot.

Erik Miller (Salisbury State '95, Division III Championship MVP) – As a pro became friends – his insight is here also.

Chet Speed (Colgate '87, Washington Lacrosse Club) - Teammate / friend who taught me by example.

Len Supko (Navy '70, Bowie Lacrosse Club) - Teammate in my early days of lacrosse.

Jim Miller (Bowie Lacrosse Club, USCLA 70's) - My teammate who played very well with no college experience.

Jonathan Marcus (Hopkins, '96) - A talented goalie at JHU who I watched a lot while writing this book.

Brian Carcaterra (Hopkins, '00) - An extremely talented goalie that taught the spirit of top level play and great saves low.

Hunter Frances (Team Toyota) - A fan of the book who has continually encouraged my writing and teaching.

John, Brian and Reed As a result of this book, I got the chance to coach Brian Carcaterra, John Horrigan and Reed Sothoron to All-American years at Hopkins and Towson respectively and to an NCAA semi-final appearance in 2001 at Rutgers – Towson vs. Princeton - quite a journey.

Coach Koudelka **Steve Koudelka** (Gettysburg All-American Goalie and Head Coach, Lynchburg College) has been an encouragement to me and a contributor to this book

Coach Pounds **Mike Pounds**, Head Lacrosse Coach at the State University of New York at Cortland, took the time to read the draft of this book. His comments improved this book and I thank him for his candor and insight.

Coach Seaman **Tony Seaman**, Head Coach at Johns Hopkins University and then Head Coach at Towson University, has had the faith to allow me to be on his staff, coaching goalies. It was an honor to work with him.

Goalie Want-a-be's When I began to coach high school lacrosse, I did not realize how much the young people gave back to me. It is the keepers I have met and coached that make the hours worthwhile. I wish that I could name you all from all the YES (NCAA Youth Education Through Sports) clinics and the camps and the smaller clinics. But, to all of you, thank you. You have shined, improved and played effectively using the techniques that I have borrowed from other successful goalies and coaches.

Ron Pramschufer of RJ Communications, LLC, the internet's self-publishing superstore (*www.selfpublishing.com*), has helped immensely in making this book an improvement over Lacrosse Goaltending for Coaches (Players Too). His publishing advise and contribution to the upgrade to our cover and graphics are much appreciated. Ron is the dad of a lacrosse goalie and has used my book in coaching in New York. Small world. Thanks to all.

Introduction

**Lacrosse -
A Great Game**

In 1964, I entered Johns Hopkins University on a academic scholarship. It was the only really good school that my family could afford. The education was excellent and I have enjoyed being an alumnus for forty years. The surprise was that Johns Hopkins is the home for an incredible, elegant, delightfully difficult field game;

LACROSSE.

I developed a love - hate relationship with the lacrosse. I loved the game and I hated how poorly I played it. I have continued to play and coach and am in awe of the sport and of people that I have met. Beyond giving back some of what I have been taught, the other purpose of this book is to re-tell a few of the stories of the game.

A Little History

In the spring of 1984, I attended a practice of the Washington Lacrosse Club (WLC) where for eight years I had been the head coach (Central Atlantic Lacrosse League, 75-83) after a mottled career as a bench warming middie and man-down defensive specialist in the United States Club Lacrosse Association (USCLA). In talking with Jeff Singer, the NCAA all-time save leader (MIT), WLC's All-Star goalie and my friend of many years, I found the team down to only one goalie, Jeff.

I lobbied to become the team's second goalie (practice goalie) if Jeff would teach me the position. I was 38 years old and had had little lacrosse success. The deciding factor was the haunting thought that I did not have a reasonable excuse to walk away. I wasn't too old or too slow. I could find the time. I loved the game and my one often-injured ankle was sound enough. So, I volunteered to be a target until I got better.

The next ten years were both frustrating and delightful as I lived up to Jeff's statement that it takes five or more years to learn to play lacrosse goalie well. But, after eight years, the lacrosse success that had eluded me for so long came around and stayed.

In 1994, when my long time friend, Geoff Berlin (Hopkins 1968 - goalie) could not make it to the Lacrosse Classic Old Timer's game (for players over 35) at Johns Hopkins, I got to start. Playing against Brooks Sweet (All World 1984) and with Jim Ulman (University of

Virginia, 1970s) and other great players, our South team won 16-8 and I was the most surprised MVP ever.

Jon and Jeff

On that performance, when Rodney Rullman moved from Ulman's Virginia Masters team to the Long Island STX team for the 1994 Vail Masters tournament, Jim Ulman asked me to play goal for them. I was MVP for one of the games (we won 4-1 and they out shot us by a bunch) and we met my usual masters team, goal tended by my teacher, Jeff Singer, in the second bracket championship. Although they won 6-5, it was a great day for goal-tenders. There were great saves and a few great goals.

JHU one time

That fall, I started at Johns Hopkins in the JHU alumni vs. JHU Varsity game that is the last game of the varsity fall ball. It was a thrill to play with Dave Petramala, Dennis Townsend, Joe Cowan and other icons of lacrosse. Others played better than I that day, but it was a wonderful to play for Hopkins that one short quarter.

World Games

In 1998, at the first ever Grand Masters (over 45 years old) championship at the World Games at Johns Hopkins, I got to play for the Championship on the U.S. Stars team that lost to a fine U.S. Eagles team 4-7 - a great day for the old guys of lacrosse. By 1999, were three national tournaments with Grand Masters play. Many of those teammates played in the 2002 World Games in Perth, Australia and in Canada in 2006.

Coaching at Magruder

In 1988, at the request of my son, Matt, I volunteered to help Arthur ("Hunky") LaMotte start a high school lacrosse program at Magruder High School, in Rockville, MD. For five years, Hunky was the general manager while we built from nothing to a winning program. Shane Murphy handled the defense while I handled offense, middies and goalies. The '92-'96 seasons (40-13 with 2 regular season championships) were rewarding as so many kids got so much out of lacrosse.

Coaching with Friends

In 1994, 1995, 1996 and 1997 at the NCAA Lacrosse Championships at University of Maryland, 1998 at Rutgers and 1999 back at Maryland, the NCAA Youth Education through Sports (NCAA YES) conducted a program where collegiate coaches, assisted by high school coaches, held free clinics for youth and high school players. Each year I enjoyed working with goaltenders and learning from college coaches: Glen Theil (Head Coach, Penn State University), Guy Van Arsdale (Head Coach, Rochester Institute of Technology and later Assistant Coach Penn State) and Mike Pounds (Head Coach, State University of New York at Cortland). Many of their thoughts are incorporated here as well.

Coaching with Seaman

In the spring of 1997, I convinced Tony Seaman, Head Coach at Johns Hopkins, then little more than a casual acquaintance, to let me come and observe his goal-keepers for one practice. If my comments helped, then he could pass them on to his players. They helped and he asked me to come back and I did.

Tony & Towson

When JHU, my alma mater, dismissed him, Tony moved to Towson. It seemed that my college coaching career was over. Then Tony startled me with an offer to join his staff as the goalie coach. It is a 136 mile round trip each day from home to work in Northern Virginia to Towson and yet to me it was delightful trip each day. Coaching with Coach Seaman, Stan Ross and Paul Cantabene was a dream come true as we built a champion program at Towson. I enjoyed all 5 years at Towson.

American U & Kendra

When one door closes another opens. I had done a little coaching in Vail of a women's club team and met Kendra King, now Kendra Burnam. Later, because of that friendship she coached at Towson and American University where she needed some help with keepers. The two years that I spent with Kendra and Ashley Flanigan were an education and a great time as we contented in the competitive Patriot League.

Back to High School

In 2007, I returned to coach high school with Tony Gray Gray at Oakton High School in Virginia. Every day on the field continues to be good

Still Playing

At this time, I still play goal, coach and teach goaltending up and down the east coast. It keeps me both humble and alive – there are not bad days on a lacrosse field, some cold/wet, but all good.

Things that Work

This book provides things that work (garnered from successful goalies and coaches). It is for all those delightful men's and women's coaches who have asked,

"What can I do to help my goalie?"

or those goalies who have asked,

"What should I do to play goal better?"

Some techniques work better than others for an individual keeper. It is important to mix in these good techniques with the goalie's own strengths. Not every technique or method is for every keeper, but the techniques here do work - proven by great keepers.

Rullman's Style   My friend and an elegant goalie, Rodney Rullman, plays with a flamboyant style. He has incredibly quick hands, great feet and eyesight. He cleanly catches each shot, cradling immediately and then with an almost sidearm flick, releases the ball up field to start the break. You would love to have Rodney on your team because he is an impact player.

But, this book does not teach Rodney's style since it is predicated on his unique and extraordinary skill. Someone might even say that Rodney is not fundamentally sound since his hands look too low, he seems to go to his knees too early, and his stick twirling even during saves seems to leave him vulnerable. His success proves his style works, for him.

Marcus' Style   As I have watched Jonathan Marcus play goal so well for Johns Hopkins in the 1990s, I have noticed that he keeps his hands quite low and his chest high using his extra-ordinary ball sense and reactions to almost explode to the shot. Jonathan is an excellent goalie that any coach would want between the pipes. But, it is rare to have the incredible reactions that he had. This book does not teach your keeper to goal tend the way he does since his saves are based on extraordinary quickness.

Learning a Style   This book does teach Rodney's excellent stance, grip and positioning. It does incorporate Jonathan's concentration and position. Other sections present a teachable style predicated upon repeatable mechanics and attitude meant to produce the high save percentages and ball management needed in a winning program. When a keeper of extraordinary quickness or other special skills strays from what is taught here, it is up to the coach to adapt to this player's special abilities.

For Men and Women   For those of you whose primary interest is in women's lacrosse, this book is also for you. Although the women's game is different on the field, goaltending is almost exactly the same for men and women. In clinics/camps we teach the women and men the same approach, techniques, tips, methods and attitudes; *because they work*. As for political correctness, instead of indicating "he/she" or "him/her" in each sentence, I have chosen the male gender and ask female readers to translate.

Not for Indoor   Indoor goaltending and field goaltending are different, except in the mental part of the game. Indoor (box lacrosse) goaltending is mostly a matter of blocking the shot with the stick, the body, pads, or whatever one can get in the way of the shot. Field lacrosse saves are made mostly with the stick. For most players, goal-tending indoors hinders the development of field skills (and vice versa). Having played both indoors and outdoors successfully, I can confidently say that this book has little to do with indoor goaltending.

For Goalies Too   Although written from a coaching perspective, it is meant to be helpful to the player also.

Let me know   If this book succeeds at helping you or if I have overlooked or miscommunicated something let me know. In addition, the Coach's Corner from our on-line www page covers topics of interest every month. Many of these comments and columns are included in this edition.

Future versions may incorporate your comments, too. Drop me a line or call:

Jon Weston
Weston Lacrosse
5920 Bethlehem Court
Rockville, MD 20855

Telephone: 301-294-3234
e-mail: Westonlax@aol.com
WWW: *www.thegoalieman.com*

CHAPTER 1
Scope

Bob Scott

Bob Scott, lacrosse coach icon at Johns Hopkins, National Hall of Fame coach and a friend of over forty years, in his landmark book, Lacrosse Technique and Tradition, 1976, made three brief statements (among many that I have read and treasured) that have stuck with me regarding goaltending.

"The goalie must be the most courageous player on the field, or some might say the craziest, because he must have no fear of being hit anywhere on his body with a solid rubber ball traveling at speeds that reach 90 miles per hour. . . . Courage and quick reactions are the most important credentials for a goalie."

"The goalie is the backbone of the team's defense and probably carries more responsibility on his shoulders than any other player on the field. There have been few championship teams, if any, with a mediocre goalie."

"Finally, and possibly just as important as courage and quick reflexes, the goalie must have <u>confidence</u> in himself. This is important to meet the challenge of the opponent's shooters and to command his own defense."

Coaches Must Coach

With courage at the center, coaches need to add the skills and attitudes needed to be successful in goal. With their importance to our teams, it is clear that leaving goalie development up to a few camp days during the summer and an occasional clinic neglects goalkeeping.

Coaches need to coach keepers every day

Without feedback, tuning and a strong relationship with one or more of the coaching staff, many goalies become inconsistent or decline in their on-field performance. With our help, they can enjoy the game and we can enjoy the success that comes with a real stopper in the crease.

Dan Mackesey and I were warming up for the Vail Masters and I saw a couple of things that I told him. He said, "It's good to have a goalie coach again". Dan proved once again that all goalies need coaches.

Teaching   This book teaches a style that involves getting the most range and smoothness out of the keeper through teaching good mechanics (hands, position, stance, steps, etc.) and through teaching attitude and concentration. The remainder of the book is organized along these lines wrapping-up with a chapter on shooting technique so that goalies can know what shooters want to do and how to deal with them and a chapter of advanced topics.

Objective   The goalie's objective is the same as the defense's:

End the opposition possession with the ball

Making saves is the most crucial way to accomplish this but a ground ball, run out, pickoff or save with no rebound are all equal since they get the ball. Saves where there are rebounds are less successful since many rebounds end in opponent scores. And it doesn't matter if the action is accomplished by the goalie or the defense. A goalie/coach should cheer the defensive as much as the goalie – they are equal.

Approach   In our clinics we emphasis 7 things where we teach:

1) **Watch the Ball -** concentration
2) **Watch the Ball with your Hand** - quickest way – your hands are faster when they are in the line of vision to the ball and your body will follow your top hand lead too
3) **Position / Readiness** - be in a great ready stance
4) **Make the save easy** – move hands, feet and chest to the ball with economy of motion and efficient speed (smoothly)
5) **Start the break** - pass very well after the save
6) **Protect the pipe** - critical to team defense
7) **Talk** - direct the D and to yourself to manage attitude

The first four are about being ready and making saves.
The last three are about key ways to contribute more.

For coaches, this book focuses first on mechanics to arm the coach with concrete technique to use immediately. As the keeper advances, then the material regarding attitude and advanced techniques can be applied to form a progression of improvement for the keeper. Lastly we look at goalkeeping at the highest level in a section on High Performance Goaltending.

CHAPTER 2
Mechanics

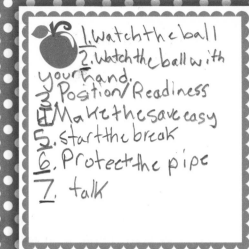

Body Management

The mechanics of goaltendin[g] keepers to do with their BOD[Y] outlet passes with a;

- **minimum of effort**
- **maximum smoothness**
- **maximum effectiveness**
- **maximum range**
- **minimum of errors**

When we teach a keeper to cover more of the goal, more easily and with less effort, he can develop better concentration and confidence for;

- **better SAVE PERCENTAGE**
- **fewer REBOUNDS**
- **more STUFFS** (unexpected saves)
- **fewer MISSES** (goals that should be saves)
- **more FAST BREAKS**
- **fewer broken CLEARS**

Technique

There are two parts to body management. The first involves technique (stance, footwork, etc.) and the second involves playing "loose".

Play Loose

I first heard this term from Dan Mackesey (Cornell '76, two time All-American and NCAA Tournament 25th Anniversary Team goalie) while we waited to play in the Vail Masters Tournament in 1996. He said that one of his major keys to good goaltending was to be prepared <u>and</u> "loose" (almost relaxed) instead of tense to move smoothly to the shot/ball and make the save. Since then, I have used this to play more effectively -- it really works. This "loose-ness" does not mean a lackadaisical attitude or lack of concentration, it just means a lack of tenseness. All the technique in this chapter is not useful if the keeper is stiff and can't move effectively during the shot. Work with the keeper to stay "loose" while learning.

Top Hand Tight In a practical sense it means the only really tense muscles are the ones that help the top hand hold the stick tight throughout the save.

Foundation Teaching effective technique is a critical foundation to good goaltending. It does not substitute for courage but it can overcome some lack of quickness or athleticism. Small change in mechanics can produce a huge improvement in range or smoothness. Teaching bad technique can damage performance.

Range Range is the area the goalie can cover during the shot. The goalie's range should be the goal area plus about 1/2 foot on each side and above the cross bar.

Teaching a goalie to save a shot that is two feet over the goal where he jumps or teaching saves where he drops to his knees for low shots is counter-productive. The keeper that has a move for one area of the goal that sacrifices his balance or coverage of another area needs to change to be less vulnerable.

Teach a consistent form that covers the whole goal smoothly and effectively and allows for quick recovery to face rebound shots.

Stepping for Range and Speed Range is developed through effective mechanics (this means speedy ones) and effective stepping. Although coaches have said for years that the keeper should step to "cut off the angle" (true) and "get behind the ball" (true), the real reason for stepping is to **"get the hands to the ball faster"**. The speedy area for the hands (sweet spot – where the hands are nearer the body) is not as large as the goal, so stepping is vital for effective range. In the figure the corners is where shooters are going.

A stance wider than the shoulders and wider than shown with toes pointed at the shooter makes stepping easy.

Hands Another example that improves range involves the hands. If they are very close together, the keeper can generate very quick rotation, but does not easily cover the whole goal. A keeper will tend to have shots go under his stick on the off side low shot.

If the hands are far apart, then the range is excellent but reactions are slowed by too much arm/shoulder movement for most saves. Perfect position is the hands a forearm length apart - 11-13 inches. length - the longer the forearm then the farther apart the hands.

*Feet more than shoulder width apart, knees
bent and hands up are vital to a good stance*

Strange Truth   Most important is the top hand position in the stance. When the
hand is at eye level (ring finger at eyebrow level), it is faster in almost
every way than if it is not clearly within the vision line to the ball.
This is easily demonstrated and true. So, not only is the 1st rule of
good goaltending to Watch the Ball, but the 2nd rule is to Watch the
Ball With Your Hand. The more that top hand sights in on the ball in
the shooters pocket and in flight the more adjustment can be made
during the shot and the faster the hands are to the shot.

Limbs Ready   The second key to range is to have all limbs ready for movement. This means knees bent, feet far apart with off-stick side foot back a little and toes pointed at the shooter, elbows bent and pointing downward, back slightly bent forward, weight on the balls of the feet, hands high with the lower hand slightly farther out than the upper hand. This is the preferred stance.

Take a Step   Brian Dougherty (Maryland '96 and two time 1st team All-American) says the third key is taking a step:

> **"You have to take a step on every shot. Shots and shooters are too fast to lay back and wait for the shot -- you must take a step toward the shot."**

Thus, the legs and whole body must be in a position to take the step moving in front of the ball and rotating the stick to the ball, high or low. Mike Pounds says that he wants the keeper to almost be off balance, falling forward toward the ball. This is really the same comment;

TAKE A STEP – Go to the ball

Why Step   Step to get your fast hand area to the ball faster. Arms are not long enough to be fast to the corners, so stepping helps to the ball faster (with fewer rebounds).

Bend   "Bent-ness" is a major factor, it's associated with "loose-ness", too. If a leg or elbow is locked (straight) then the body is rigid and cannot move effectively or quickly. If the back is straight up and down (perpendicular to the ground), then the shoulders cannot rotate down to the low shot without first bending the back (slow). If the elbow is straight then stick rotation is restricted until the elbow is bent. Start bent - stay quick.

Range is first obtained by a stance that has all the limbs ready for movement to the ball and all the body parts positioned to make the move efficiently.

Smoothness   Range and smoothness go together. The smoother the move (fewer, shorter, fluid movements), the more repeatable it is and the more effective it is with little wasted motion. Avoiding that provides time to get to shots that are farther away (generating a greater range). The key to smoothness is avoiding initial movement(s) before moving to the ball. For example;

• A keeper that steps to a stick side high shot with upper body still while shot is saved, that's smooth.

- If he steps to an off-side high shot and moves the top hand across his face and bottom in front of the top hand forearm to make the save, that is smooth.
- If the keeper steps toward the ball, rotates the hands to make the save on the low shot, that is smooth.

Wasted Motion If the keeper has to move a foot, prior to stepping toward the ball, or raise his hands prior to rotating the stick to the ball, or take two steps to be in position, then the wasted motion is <u>not</u> smooth and takes time.

Shot Speed		Distance from Goal and Speed Determines Seconds from Shooter to Save (0.25 = ¼ second)						
MPH	Yds / sec	8 yds	9 yds	10 yds	11 yds	12 yds	13 yds	14 yds
90	44.0	0.18	0.20	0.23	0.25	0.27	0.30	0.32
80	39.1	0.20	0.23	0.26	0.28	0.31	0.33	0.36
70	34.2	0.23	0.26	0.29	0.32	0.35	0.38	0.41
60	28.3	0.27	0.31	0.34	0.38	0.41	0.44	0.48

0.25 to 0.48 second is the time available to make the save.

Wasted Time Wasted time is the goaltenders enemy. This wasted time. means some shots are going in that shouldn't have. The table above shows the amount of time that goalie has from the time the shot leaves the stick until he makes the save (for example there are $23/100^{ths}$ of a second to make react to a 90 mile per hour shot at 10 yards).

The best goalies cannot react in less than a 1/5 of a second (0.20 seconds) and even top goalies are hard pressed to make any good move in less than 1/4 of a second (0.25 seconds). It is important for the defense to keep the shooters from shooting hard close in and for the keeper to have the quickest (and smoothest) reactions.

Putting this another way, for a shot going 90 miles per hour (44 yards per second), the wasting of 1/10 of a second by the keeper means that the shooter can beat the keeper from four yards farther out. **This means that the defense has to defend an area that is twice as large (300 square yards vs. 150 square yards) as would normally be defended (14 yards out instead of 10 yards out).**

Goalie concentration and smoothness that saves that 1/10 second makes defense easier.

Smoothness is based on position, mechanics, readiness and

concentration (watching the ball). If the keeper is out of position and has to lunge across the goal to have a chance at the save, he will have very few options (little range) during the lunge and will not be smooth -- lowering the chance of adjusting to the shot and of making the save. But, if the position is good (he is in between the shooter and the goal), the stance is good and he is tracking the ball with his top hand then the keeper can calmly step to the ball and make the save smoothly (and quickly).

Rebounds

There is another factor involving smoothness. The smoother the save attempt, the less chance of a rebound. The more the keeper has to jump or stab or bat or kick at the ball to make the save then the higher chance of the ball bounding back out toward the offense. Rebounds are the most dangerous of the unsettled situations that produce goals. When the keeper can cut down on rebounds there are less scoring chances.

Mechanics

Mechanics is what the keeper does with his body parts to prepare for and execute the key actions of a goaltender. Good mechanics help the keeper be effective. Mechanics is not position (where the keeper is in relation to the play - see Chapter III). Mechanics involves Stance, Position, Saves, Catching and Throwing, all covered below.

The remainder of this chapter is devoted to teaching good mechanics.

A Stance

Fluidity

The purpose of learning a stance is to prepare to have all the hands, limbs and trunk moving smoothly and quickly during the shot / save. This means having a comfortable and aggressive stance maintained with joints bent where the keeper can readily move to any area of the goal.

Grip

It starts with the grip:

- **STICK rotation is critical to saves**
- **WRIST rotation is critical to stick rotation**
- **HAND position/GRIP is critical to wrist rotation.**

This means having the wrists to the back of shaft so that both wrists can rotate as the stick rotates.

**Chicken Wings
Bad Form**

Occasionally, one will see a goaltender set up so that the whole back of both gloves (fingers, glove back and wrist guard) are visible to the shooter. Wide or up elbows may accompany this grip. We call this "chicken wings".

This grip significantly restricts stick rotation to all corners of the goal. The wrists can't turn much and shoulders have to move to move the hands very far (too slow).

Good Grip The top knuckle portion of the fingers should be visible to the shooter (wrists to the back of the shaft) and the elbows should point down (not out) to allow easy moves low or windshield wiper move to off-stick side high.

As shown in the figure the keeper grips the stick, especially with the top hand, different from field players. He grips the stick between the top part of the thumb and the bottom part of the forefinger with the thumb gripping the flat side of the stick and the forefinger base gripping the opposite flat side of the stick (so that all the fingers could be pointing at the shooter if they were straight). The forefinger is then wrapped around to the thumb. The stick is gripped with only the thumb and forefinger and second finger. The other fingers loop around the stick to the front so that they are not injured if hit by the shot. These fingers do not grip the stick (ring and pinky).

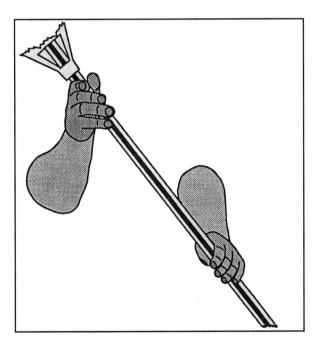

Top hand grips the stick tight between thumb and two top fingers.
Bottom hand grips loosely almost a loop grip.

*Wrists to the back of the shaft, elbows pointing
down toward just outside the toes*

With this grip the ball is not caught in a cradling motion. The
objective is to get the ball to hit the pocket and after making the stop
get fuller control of the ball. If the elbows are bent a little at impact
there is no need to cradle catch or give with the shot, the arms will
do it automatically

No Rebound   With the shaft OFF THE PALM, a result is the softness in the hands
when the ball is saved - minimizes rebounds.

One Detail   Make sure that the wrist remains in the correct position for full stick
rotation (both wrists to the back of the shaft). It is easy to slip the
thumb to the back of the stick or to slide the index finger knuckles
around to the front of the stick. Either change forms a very poor
grip. Re-enforce the importance of the position the wrist to the back
of the shaft and in gripping the stick with the thumb and top two
fingers (not the picky and ring fingers – restricts wrist rotation). And
GRIP the stick with the top hand (tightly) – this helps in the accuracy
of moving to the shot.

**Gripping
the Throat**   Some goalies with big hands grip the throat of the stick (not the
shaft). It takes big hands to use this technique and even then grip

restricts stick rotation. The preferred top hand grip is on the shaft wrist to the shaft back .

Hands too close together are fast but restrict range

Hand Placement   The motion used in saving involves ROTATING the stick. Top hand is next to the plastic. The bottom hand is placed below the top hand as the rotation the pivot point. As the stick rotates, the wrists provide pivot points for the stick. A grip with the thumb and top two fingers allows the wrist/stick rotation for more than 180 degrees (one half turn). We need to rotate the stick 270 to 360 degrees (3/4 turn to a full turn). Wrists at the back of the shaft and top two fingers grip allow this rotation.

Hands too Close   If hands are close together, then the stick can be rotated quickly but it doesn't cover the whole goal (see figure above) making the keeper vulnerable low.

Hands too Far   If the hands are too far apart, then the range may be better but the increased arm/shoulder arm movement makes the keeper slower and vulnerable to hard shots, especially on off-stick side saves.

Best Hands   A compromise is used. Range is enhanced by a short step to the shot, so the compromise is more toward good stick rotation with knees bent for good stepping.

The best position leaves the hands 8-12 inches apart (actually one forearm length apart).

Hands to far apart slows down movement to the ball

Stick Taping   Taping the stick provides friction with the face of the glove. Since
the top hand holds the stick tight, it helps keep a hard shot hitting the
plastic from rotating the stick head on impact. Tape nubs re-enforces
hand placement. The first nub of tape is just below the stick throat.
This provides a home place for the top hand. One nub is put 16-18
inches below the head to position the bottom hand. A third nub is
put on the end so that the stick stops when the keeper slides the stick
up to pick off a high pass

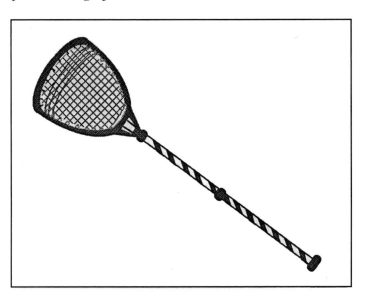

Tape aids grip and hand placement

Hands and Eyes When I was at soccer goalie camp, learning to play / coach soccer goaltending with my son, the instructor said something important regarding keeping one's hands up in front of his face and between his face and the ball;

"As the hands move toward the ball, the body will follow"

It is the same in lacrosse.

Eye-Thumb-Ball If the top hand thumb is just to the side of a line between the eyes and the ball between, the body will follow the hands for the save. I call this:

EYE - THUMB - BALL !!

It may sound silly, but it works. At our camp, we use "Eye-Thumb-Ball" or **"Watch the Ball with you HAND"** to remind the goalies to keep them concentrating on this relationship. This is useful on shots, but as important, it works on passes too. By watching the ball using the hand, the body is in position earlier than if the head moves and the body follows.

Hands Off Chest There is a lot of physiology involved with eye-thumb-ball. To do it the keeper must significantly extend his arms so that his elbows are out in front of the chest (for all save motions). This allows freedom of movement and enhances the reactions on high shots in close.

Avoid Loading-up Not only does the keeper move fluidly with his hands and eyes coordinated in a line to the ball, but also he avoids "loading-up". A keeper with his hands too low, has to "load-up" to be ready for the shot (by bringing his hands and the stick into a better or higher position). By "looking-beside-the-thumb" the delay caused by "loading-up" is avoided (keeper is already "loaded" with hands and eyesight in line) and goaltending is improved.

A critical part about the hands is that the more they top hand starts high (up just to one side of the top hand eye), the quicker and more fluid the hands and body are to the ball. This quickness and smoothness is what we are striving for to improve the keeper's game.

Letting the keeper cheat by keeping his hands low or close to the chest really hurts timing, ability to concentrate and fosters "stabbing" at the ball (produces rebounds). Working with the keeper to "watch the ball with the hand" not only helps his concentration and smoothness but gives the coach a simple piece of advice when the keeper needs to reset his concentration during a game (**Hands Up**).

Feet and Legs

The feet need to be shoulder width or more apart with the toes pointed inward just a bit. This pigeon-toed stance allows the keeper to push off with the off ball foot without having to move the foot. If the off-side foot (the one on the other side of the body from the shot) is a little slew-footed then the keeper must move and plant it prior to pushing off for the step with the other foot during the shot. This re-planting of the off-side foot wastes time and interferes with a good smooth reaction to the shot. Slew-foot may cost a couple of goals a game, where a pigeon-toed stance may gain an extra save or two a game.

Footwork

Footwork is important – it makes turns on passes, cross-crease and from behind and stepping to shots effective. Footwork on saves means pushing your hips, chest and hands to the ball simultaneously with moving your hands. The pigeon-toed stance technique and playing on the balls of the feet (not the heels), provides smooth movement to the ball when the keeper "takes a step" on each shot extending quickness and range.

One Foot Forward

The legs need to be bent at the knee with feet more than shoulder width apart. Either the feet need to be about even or the lead/top hand foot a couple inches in front of the other foot. The top hand on the stick is the lead hand. For a right handed goalie, the right hand is the lead hand and the lead foot is the right foot. The keeper pushes off differently than a pitcher using the off-ball foot to push the hips to push the hands to the ball faster.

The right foot (lead foot) is forward a bit for balance and to minimize interference with the left knee when rotating the stick to make the off-stick side save. More weight is placed on the lead foot, not less (as a way of getting the keeper onto the balls of both feet). On the off-side high shot, the bottom end of the stick passes directly in front of the left knee. On the off-side low shot, the top end of the stick passes directly in front of the left knee (going in other direction).

If the non-lead foot is back a little, the keeper misses hitting the knee with the stick on either save. Having one foot a little ahead of the other makes getting low for low shots much easier yielding better range and smoothness.

The clear threat in this stance is that the one foot will be back so far that it hinders mobility to one side or another. By making it back just a little mobility is not compromised. In any case, the keeper must extend his hands far enough from the chest for clear rotation of the stick without hitting either knee.

If the keeper has good balance and mobility with his feet even then work with him that way. If not, look to move the lead foot forward with feet wide and a little pigeon toed – toes pointing at the shooter or a little inward. Having toes inward supports the off-ball foot push of the body to the ball as the ball-side foot steps.

"STAND TALL" makes it easy for the shooter to shoot around the keeper – use a full stance instead

Bending the Legs Bending the legs is vital. Many goals where a keeper misses or where a rebound results are because one or both legs are locked - not bent. When a leg is straight (locked) then the keeper cannot move quickly and a rigid body contributes to stiff hands also.

This is so fundamental that it means LOSING in every goaltender I have seen. With bent legs, the keeper's mobility and range is best.

Get Your Butt Down All keepers get locked legs occasionally. So teach them to get their "**Butt Down**" and they will bend the legs. Some keepers, especially short ones, complain that they think they are leaving the upper part of the goal open unless they stand tall (with straight legs as shown in figure on prior page). A full stance with hands high (eye level) supports more range while still covering the goal

Rock and Kick An advanced form of bad footwork is called Rock-and-Kick where the keeper rocks back on the back foot and then kicks the front foot toward the shot usually landing that foot heel first. This is a neat looking style move BUT it limits range, especially low, and is SLOW (you have to rock back before going forward a limited distance).

Bottom Hand Forward not Back As shown in the figure below, the bottom hand is forward of the top hand with both hands out from the chest enough to avoid the stick from hitting the knees (or elbows brushing the chest) when the stick is rotated. For high, hard shots, this means very controllable saves. If the top hand is farther out than the bottom then two bad things happen;

1) rebounds caused by stabbing at high shots,
2) rebounds caused by the stick in the "scooping" position on the low shots

Chest is in front of the hips so that the shoulders can rotate especially to low / bounce shots

Rebounds come from the ball hitting the stick stop and bouncing out of the stick. As the ball hits the net with the face tilted slightly back, the ball stays in the stick or bounces up softly taking the power out of the shot allowing the keeper time to "corral" the ball. Likewise, the bottom hand forward on a low shot keeps the ball from bouncing out of the crease back to the offense.

This is not a dramatic tilting of the stick, just a little so that the most stick area is facing the shot. It is important that the top hand be in front of the helmet so that the keeper can "eye-thumb-ball" site the ball and move the stick in front of the helmet for the off-side save. The key here is that the keeper has much less control when the head is tilted forward (more rebounds) and much more with the stick head a little back. By keeping the elbows bent, there is natural give to the shock of the ball hitting the pocket this combined with the bounce from the stick being back a little minimizes rebounds.

Hands in Front   Coach Pounds, Cortland State, and Coach Thiel, Penn State, both teach that the hands and elbows are in front of the chest on all saves from setup until the ball is in the pocket. Having the bottom hand out from the chest facilitates this for all moves.

*Start in a baseball shortstop's stance,
lift up to an aggressive goalie's stance*

Getting into Your Stance   Getting into a good stance is easy. Use this simple setup: Start in the stance a baseball shortstop uses (feet more than shoulder width apart--a bit pigeon-toed, knees bent, butt down, back bent and forearms on the thighs) then raise the hands and back up almost in a fighters stance. Start as shown in the figure and then raise up the hands, shoulders and butt. Careful, there is no time when the goalie should stay in this very deep crouch during play. This is one way to get into a normal stance.

Little Differences Little changes can bring big improvements. One small change of raising the stick and changing its initial position a little toward horizontal helps some goalies move more smoothly to more places.

*Top hand high and bottom hand lower helps
both high and low saves*

*High hands helps from having to load up –a practice stance
then drop the bottom hand some*

Stance Summary A save is a save and there is no perfect or correct technique. But,
some are more effective than others. All saves are not created equal.
If the save results in a rebound then a goal is likely. So, technique that
gets both the save and the ball is valuable.

Stance and position are the parts of the save that can be done before
the shot that increase save percentages.

Stance is one place to be better prepared prior to having to react smoothly and quickly to make the save.

B. Saves

Save Areas

Making saves isn't easy but a keeper can control three things;

1) **Watch** the ball continuously on passes and from the shooters pocket into the goalie stick pocket – using the top hand as a sight to the ball
2) **Ready** to make the save in his/her best stance
3) **Go**-ing to the shot by driving the top & bottom hands toward the ball and by pushing the hips and chest to the ball while stepping

Attacking the Shot

There are three modes of goaltending:

1) passive position – ineffective against good shooters
2) reactive - partially effective but late many times
3) attacking - most effective.

Attacking means driving the hands to the ball and pushing the body forward to help get the hands to the ball faster. The objective of warm-ups is to move the keeper quickly through to attacking (from catching, to better stance and rotation to stepping and smothering the shot). Teach the keeper to move up from catching to reacting to attacking as he learns to be a goal keeper.

Take a STEP, Every Time

It almost can't be said enough or too often:

TAKE A STEP TOWARDS EVERY SHOT

Stepping gets the hands to the ball faster

The first step is taken with the ball side and is driven by a push from the off-ball side foot to move the hips and chest forward pushing the hands to the ball. There are two schools of stepping; One Step and Three.

One Step

One long step is better than not stepping and for very big goalies it has been effective (Brian "Doc" Doughtery or Pat McGinnis of University of Maryland).

Triple Step   For most goalies, one step means slowing down too soon or not
                         getting far enough to make the save quickly. The preference is the
                         triple step:

                         1) one short step with the ball side foot with a push by the back side
                            foot to move the hips forward
                         2) a quick step with the off-ball foot
                         3) followed immediately by the reset of the ball side foot

                         The 2nd and 3rd steps returns the keeper to the balanced, on-the-balls-
                         of-the-feet stance that he/she began with If the shot is stick-side or
                         right at the keeper, the right-handed keeper steps with the right foot.
                         If it is an off-side shot then the step is with the left foot. The keeper
                         needs to have weight on the balls (not the heels) of both feet for
                         either step (left or right) to be in time and effective.

                         The step is best taken with the foot pointed at the shooter. It may
                         seem good to throw the foot out to the side a bit to cover just under
                         the stick, but this turns the stick to the side making saves harder.

                         Stepping is vital and part of attacking the shot. If a goalie is on his
                         heels during or after a shot, then he is not attacking the shot (not
                         stepping) and is getting beat unnecessarily. Re-enforce playing on the
                         balls of the feet and stepping to the shot in warm-up and in games.
                         If the keeper gets stationary, remind him to step to the shot.

                         After taking a step to the shot and making the save then the rear foot
                         is brought forward to form a balanced stance to either corral the ball
                         or throws the outlet pass.

Save Areas   Each save area has a name:

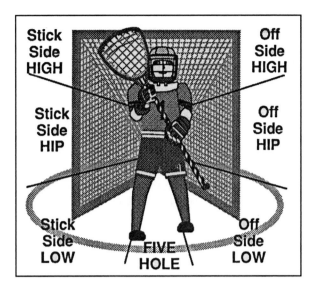

The goalie learns moves for each area of the goal

Saving Versus   One thing should be clear: the first objective on a shot is to save the
Catching   ball. After that, the keeper corrals the ball and makes the throw that
starts the fast break.

Trying to catch the shot turns the stick and
lowers the chance of saving it

Making saves for each save type, we are using a propeller motion
(not a catching motion as in the figure above). Catching is something
the field players do or keepers do when they are catching a pass.
Keepers make saves with the stick face flat to the ball/shooter using
the largest area of the stick to cover the goal. The keeper should

NOT try to catch the shot, especially if that means turning the stick (cradling catch).

The objective of the movements during a shot is to STOP THE SHOT from going in the highest percentage of the time. If the stick, hands, wrists (to the shaft back) and elbows (bent) are in the correct position on high shots the stick will almost catch the ball. If one turns the stick, as a middie might do, in a flowing motion that ends in a cradle, there are times when the stick face is not fully facing the shot - lowers chances of making the save.

See it from the Side

The figure below shows the correct stance from the side. With the stick angled slightly back, when the ball hits the stick it will bounce up a little and then back in the stick.

Likewise, if the ball strikes the stick as shown in the next figure on a bounce shot, it will hit the pocket and come to rest on the ground just below the stick.

The ball will bounce and come to rest in the pocket.

Elbows in Front

The idea is to rotate the stick to the ball (and take a step towards the shot), then the hands and elbows must stay in front of the chest throughout these maneuvers.

The most frequently observed bad habits are;

a) not taking a step -- discussed above, and
b) not rotating the stick for the off-side save.

The most common form of "not rotating" is where the keeper

takes his lower hand / elbow and slides it behind his hip forming a scooping positioning for the lower off-side save. This move's only obvious flaw is that it gives up rebounds, it also ruins good rotation for the 5 hole (between the legs), on-side low and off-side hip saves.

The bottom hand provides the most speed to the ball if it is used as the lever hand that causes the rotation of the stick's propeller motion. For the off-side high save, this means pushing the bottom hand toward the on-side hip. For the low save, it means pushing the bottom hand up and across in front of the facemask (being a pivot point).

This stops the keeper from sliding his elbow and bottom hand to the side of his hip. As the keeper learns this move, speed and accuracy improve. This is what is meant by "keeping the elbows in front of the chest".

Corralling the Ball

Keepers do not "catch" a shot, they make a save. After the save, the keeper needs to gain control of the ball and prepare for the next action. The best corralling technique is bringing the stick with the ball in front of the chest with the stick head facing upwards and the ball in the pocket. If the ball bounces around some then it will hit the keeper's chest and drop back into the stick or onto the ground in front of the keeper

Corralling the ball to the chest keeps the ball from bouncing into the net after the save

High saves and hip level saves use the same final move so that the keeper's body is between the ball and the goal as he finishes the save. If the shot is low, where it hits the net and drops to the ground then it should be covered with the stick until it can be scooped.

**Stick-side
High Saves**

With a strong stance and good concentration, stick side high saves are easy:

- Look beside-the-thumb at the ball (Eye-Thumb-Ball)
- Alert the defense with a strong, "SHOT" call.
- Take a step toward the shot (stick-side foot) and push the body in back of the hands with the off-side foot
- Move the stick in front of the ball
- Let the ball hit the pocket (without trying to cradle it)
- Corral the ball and control it in the stick
- Alert the defense with a strong "CLEAR" call.
- Change the hands and stance for throwing.

Stick side high saves are easy - the basic stance sets it up. The keeper is closer to the short side post – protect-ing the pipe and forcing the shooter to the harder "long side" post (giving the keeper more reaction time).

*Off-side high saves involve rotating the stick
combined with a strong step to the ball.*

**Off-side
High Saves**

Once a keeper gets comfortable in his stance, off-side high saves are very easy. They are just like stick side high saves except that the top hand is moved across the facemask (elbow at chin level) and the bottom hand moves across in front of the top hand forearm, placing the stick on the off-side (see figure above). The step are:

- Look beside-the-thumb at the ball (Eye-Thumb-Ball)
- Alert the defense with a strong, "SHOT" call.
- Take a step toward the shot (off-side foot) and push the body in back of the hands with the off-ball foot

- Push the top hand across the facemask to move the stick head to the off-side, at the same time move the bottom hand toward the top hand elbow to effect a rotation of the stick into the off-side area.
- Move the stick in front of the ball
- Let the ball hit the pocket (without trying to cradle it)
- Corral (control) the ball in the stick
- Alert the defense with a strong "CLEAR" call
- Change the hands and stance for throwing.

For the off-side save, corralling the ball can be done by continuing the stick motion in a looping action that twists the stick face so that the keeper is looking into the pocket at the ball as the stick returns to the stick side of the keeper. Then the ball is corralled by bringing it to the front of the chest. The same idea is used for corralling that is discussed under stick side saves--bring the ball to the chest and then prepare for the outlet pass.

There is a tendency to try to "catch" the ball on the off-side high shot. Let the stick do the work on this save. If the stick head is placed on the off-side and the ball hits the pocket, the stick almost catches the ball itself. Try it. The keeper will realize that off-side high saves do not take a lot of fancy moves.

It is important on the off-side save for the keeper to not be pulled away from the stick side post too soon. The mechanics discussed here yield a very fast reaction to the high off-side shot. It is not necessary to leave the basic stance early. If the keeper moves early on this shot, the next shot attempt the shooter may fake to move the keeper a little and then come back to stick side. By using these techniques (smooth, controlled stick rotation) the keeper needn't over-anticipate the off side shot.

Stick-side Hip Saves

The hip save stick-side is very straightforward if the keeper is watching the ball and takes a step. The save is so easy that occasionally keepers get beat on stick-side hip shots because they don't do all the fundamentals. Most stick-side hip shots that go in go in because the keeper was distracted or tried to "catch" the shot instead of "make the save" and then "corral" the ball.

Since this shot is between the shin and the shoulder, it is almost natural to try to "catch" this shot. But, the correct approach is to keep the whole face of the stick in front of the ball until the ball strikes the pocket;

- Look over-the-thumb at the ball (Eye-Thumb-Ball)
- Alert the defense with a strong, "SHOT" call.
- Take a step toward the shot (stick-side foot)

- Move the stick in front of the ball
- Let the ball hit the pocket (without trying to cradle it)
- Drop the top hand to the hip and move the bottom hand to the off-side to rotate the stick to the stick-side hip area. If the ball is at knee level or lower then the bottom hand is pushed from the off-side hip up, past and in front of the chin forcing even more stick rotation while the top hand is used as a pivot (looped fingers) and a guide
- Corral (control) the ball by bringing the stick head to the belt/lower chest with the stick face facing up.
- Alert the defense with a strong "CLEAR" call
- Change the hands and stance for throwing.

Off-side Hip Saves

The off-side hip save is the hardest save to make consistently. It requires the most practice and discipline and the quickest decision made by the keeper. If the ball is at lower chest or above, then the save is made as an off-side high save. If the ball is at the belt or lower, then the off-side hip save is made as an off-side low save with more stick rotation.

The best way to teach this save is to work the keeper a lot on high shots until his limits on off-side high saves is clear. Then, work for a long time on low saves both stick-side and off-side. By extending the range of these two saves, the off-side hip save moves will develop.

There is a tendency to slide the bottom hand toward or behind the off-side hip and make the off-side low and off-side hip save in sort of a receding shovel motion. This is not recommended, since it gives up a lot of rebounds.

Coach Mike Pounds, Coach Glen Theil and others teach that good goaltending involves keeping the elbows, forearms and hands in front of the chest (using more of a propeller motion). By working on the low saves with this motion, the shovel type move can be avoided.

One key to off-side hip saves is to step more towards the pipe as the keeper steps towards the ball. This puts the hip, thigh and stomach in front of the ball. For many keepers, this is the key to this save. If the hands are a little late then the keeper makes the save with the body.

Stick-side Low Saves

The stick side low save is a continuation of the stick-side hip save, in that, the propeller action is continued so that the stick is straight up and down with the top of the stick head touching the ground as the save is made. The key to low saves is getting the keeper's butt low early so that all this stick rotation is easy and fast. If the keeper bends from the waist with straight or nearly straight legs, low shots will go in. Likewise, if the stick is not fully rotated shots can go under the stick and into the goal.

Palms Up   Notice that a full rotation low renders the palms visible as the stick goes vertical. This position of the hands after the save is an excellent indication of good grip and good rotation technique.

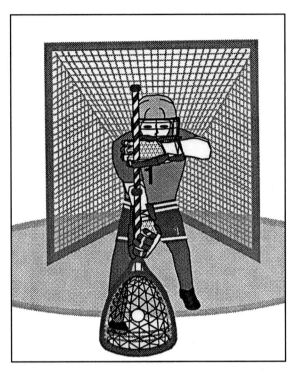

Low saves involve full stick rotation and a step
towards where the ball is to bounce

Hands   If the hands are too close together or the back is straight up and down then the rotation on the low shot will leave a gap between the stick and the ground. Most keepers try to compensate by then pushing the stick to the ground. This can be slow and the keeper is beat. An easier adjustment is to separate the hands more (still keeping the top hand as close to the stick throat as possible) and starting with the chest in front of the hips. This is quicker and brings the stick head closer to the ground on low shots during the stick rotation and the gap will be gone.

Off-side Low Saves   On the stick-side, the full stick rotation is not, in itself, the only way to make a low save. But, on the off-side, a full rotation is vital since it is the only method that consistently gets the stick in front of the low corner shot;

- Look beside-the-thumb at the ball
- Alert the defense with a strong, "SHOT" call.
- Take a step toward the shot (off-side foot)
- Move the stick in front of the ball

- Let the ball hit the pocket (without trying to catch it).
- Drive the top hand to the off-side hip then in front of the shin, at the same time move the bottom hand forward and up toward the chin to effect a rotation of the stick into the off-side low area just in <u>front</u> of the off-side foot. Use looped fingers to assure easiest and fastest rotation. If the stick is angled forward then the ball rolls to a stop at the keeper's feet.
- Corral the ball usually by picking it up off the ground and then bringing the stick head to the chest.
- Alert the defense with a strong "CLEAR"
- Change the hands and stance for throwing.

On the low save let the ball hit the pocket

Five Hole Saves   The shot that is supposed to go between the keeper's legs (Five Hole) is just another low shot and should be played as such. For keepers that are using a full stick rotation on low shots, that same move should be used with Five Hole. Once mastered, the legs should stay wide, wider than the stick so if the ball hits off the stick plastic it may hit the shin, keeping the ball out of the goal.

Some keepers don't use a full rotation on stick-side or five hole shots. These keepers tend to get the stick at a 45 degree angle to the ground and rely on hand-eye coordination to get the stick face to the ball. They may back up their stick with the leg (thigh, bent knee and calf) much like a shortstop backs up a grounder with his back leg. I prefer the full stick rotation since it is faster and covers more shots. But, if the keeper is using the other technique, it helps to body block behind the stick.

Close-in Pipe Saves High

Attackmen like to get the ball in close and try to power it past the keeper high. For these saves, I recommend staying between the pipes until the last moment and then meeting the ball as close to the shooter as possible (take a strong SINGLE step at the shooter). And;

**Never get beat between you and the pipe --
that is where the shooter wants to shoot**

Knocking the shooter down usually takes the keeper out of the play for subsequent action. By continuing to play the ball and then driving through it usually ends up in save or a "rejection" from the immediate area.

Ball Behind Moves

Whenever the ball is out in front of the goal then the keeper should face the ball to STEP toward the shot.When the ball is behind the goal, the keeper is positioned differently; he faces the ball between the pipes and one pivot step from the pipe. Almost every feed from behind or shot from the shooter driving from behind can be covered by the goalie by using TWO STEPS:

1) One pivot STEP to the PIPE (just outside the pipe) on the side where the shooter (or feed) goes - watching the ball and covering the near pipe
2) An ADDITIONAL STEP toward the shooter For feeds, this second step is taken toward where the ball is landing thus adjusting for where the feed is going. It also assures a more attacking approach (instead of stepping to the PIPE and STOPPING, the keeper continues his motion toward the player who is being fed).

Looking around the post to a player behind the goal leaves the off-side pass open (see the chapter on Positioning). Thus, facing the behind player and using the Two Step Pivot provides better goal coverage, better balance and better aggressiveness to the shot.

Pipe Saves

When the shooter comes around from behind or comes at the goal from the goal line extended, the goalie sets up so that the post nearest the shooter is covered. The shooter wants to shoot between the near pipe and the goalie. As the shooter comes around more, and can see more of the goal, the keeper has decisions to make.

The main decision to make is to STAY AT HOME (stay close to the pipe) and guard that near pipe area for even longer than the keeper thinks is prudent. If the shooter has to change his shot to go past the keeper to the long pipe side then often the shooter will miss the goal.

And, the keeper has more TIME to make the save (since the ball goes farther before hitting the net).

The first of two techniques to deal with this is to stay close to the pipe until the shooter shoots toward the long pipe and then step to the ball and shooter for the save. The second technique is called "Down-the-Line". It is covered in Advanced Techniques.

Some keepers will lean on the pipe taking them out of a good athletic stance. This impedes good movement to the ball. The stance is the same on the pipe or on shots from up field with legs bent, hips in front of the pipe and top hand at eye level pointing at the ball.

This Shot, Last Shot, Next Shot

Another key to saves is attitude. Managing attitude as a keeper is vital, but there _are_ highs and lows. The best goaltenders believe that they are going to stop every shot. But, reality is some go in and even some go in where the keeper should have made the save (others go in because the offense BEATS the defense).

None-the-less, the keeper needs to be just as confident, ready and effective on the play after a shot that goes in as he is when he makes the save (or any upbeat time):

Don't let the results of the LAST SHOT, adversely effect the preparation and performance on the NEXT SHOT.

This mental toughness can be taught. Talk it up with the goalie -- "Get ready for the next one".

At the end of normal goalie warm-ups we often put game pressure on the keeper by feeding from behind or across the front of the goal at close range and shooting. This drill makes him move and concentrate. It also produces both good reactions/ techniques and a "recoverable" attitude, since some close-in shots are saved. By re-enforcing the good saves and techniques and "shaking off" the goals and errors, the goalie learns the mental control needed to be effective in the game.

C. Throwing

There are two types of throws that a keeper makes. The first is a quick and short (less than 15 yards) pass to a clearly open teammate. This pass can be done from the keeper's regular save stance once it is learned. The second involves throwing the ball with more authority and farther (greater than 10-15 yards) and is done from a more traditional throwing stance.

Short Pop   I call the short pass a "short pop" pass. It is opportunistically thrown a short distance with the hands only (no larger arm and leg motion used in longer throws). The advantage of the short pop is that it is done very quickly to start the break.

It is executed by taking the top hand back and pushing the bottom hand out with the stick straight up and down (hands are still 10-12 inches apart and grip is still the same as used in saving the ball). By pulling the bottom hand to the elbow of the top hand arm, an accurate short throw can be done effectively.

Longer Throw   The keeper's feet and hands during a save are not in good position to throw the ball after the save. By changing to a throwing stance after the save, more accuracy, distance, power and control are gained.

A consistent, powerful, accurate and long throw is vital to goalkeeping especially with the men's lacrosse rule that requires the ball be cleared into the offensive box within 20 seconds of gaining possession. Thus, passing the ball up field accurately to at least the midline is crucial.

There are two throwing forms. One is a power throw where the top hand pushes hard and the bottom hand moves little. The other is a shooter-like motion - described below.

Throw Stance   The figure on the left shows the throwing stance. There are changes compared to the saving stance.

- The hips, chest and feet are pointing perpendicular to the line of flight of the ball (e.g. toward the sideline)
- The stick shaft is pointed toward the target (at the beginning and end of the throw).
- The bottom hand is on the butt end and the top hand is 12-16 inches above that (farther down than shown in the grip in the 2 figures – that high grip is used for a quick outlet after a save)

Throwing   To throw, the keeper's weight is transferred to the rear foot (rock back) and then moved forward by pushing with the rear foot leg and striding with the front leg. At the same time bring both hands forward driving the shaft toward the target and then pull down with the front hand (and guiding with the rear or top hand). The stick is driven forward toward the receiver just as the front hand pulls down toward the top hand elbow. The front hand finishes at or just inside the rear hand elbow with the stick head now pointing at the receiver. This overhand throw is superior to side arm since the pull down supplies the power and the overhand motion keeps the ball on line to the receiver, just like shooting overhand.

For most throws, front/bottom hand does NOT go across the front of the body (finishing behind that side hip as it done on the power throw). The stick bottom and top finish on the same side of the keeper's body. In teaching this, have the keeper almost point his butt (backside) at the receiver, thus gathering the rear foot under the body for the best push off. Do not point the lead toe at the receiver, since this opens up the hips and pulls the forward hand across the front of his chest (less effective). Keep the toes pointed perpendicular to the throw.

The stick is doing the work through the same whip effect (and pivot of the stick through the top hand) used by better shooters. And, the keeper can use his back to shield from a check while still retaining power and accuracy (much like an attackman does when pressured). If the keeper is throwing "across his chest" or "side-arm" work with him to change to this technique for improvements in accuracy, power and distance.

*Throwing the ball long and accurately
starts with the stance*

*Finish with the hands on one side of the body --
it's accurate and protects the keeper from checks.*

Throwing Rules When throwing the ball from inside the crease there is an "interference" rule that protects the goalie. Once the goalie has control, he is protected from being checked until he exits the crease. This includes contact by a defender on the goalie's follow through of the pass. Thus, if the offensive team pressures the goal keeper, he can throw the ball so that his follow through strikes the offensive player, then his team can get the ball. If the pass is completed, there is no whistle. If not, the defense gets a "free clear" (with the ball at the mid-line). Once the keeper leaves the crease this rule is not in force.

Drills

Keepers should participate in team throwing and catching drills to build their confidence and skills in working the ball during clears. In addition, have another player outside the box, at the off-stick side box corner and make the keeper throw the ball there after each warm-up or workout save. This overcomes the natural tendency to throw up the stick side of the field and gets the multiple looks (left, middle and right) desired to find the open man for the breakout clear.

Wall Ball

Goalies should work on the wall too to improve their ball handling and throwing skills. A hundred throws to the wall every day - 70 righty and 30 lefty for a righty goalie – will bring improvement in ball handling. Make at least half of these throws beyond 30 yards.

Outlet Passes

Good coaches teach the defensive players to do a "banana" cut (a long sweeping turn) toward the sideline from the crease to above the corner of the box (men) or above the 30 (women) with their stick in position to catch and "over the shoulder" catch. Since the riding player is cutting off the middle of the field, an over the shoulder outside pass to a banana cut is almost impossible to stop. The goalie knows when it will work by watching the riding player. If the rider looks at the cutting player, throw the ball, the rider won't see it. If the rider looks back to the keeper either throw to someone else or wait for the clearing player to back cut the rider (back to the middle) for an open pass and clear path to the goal.

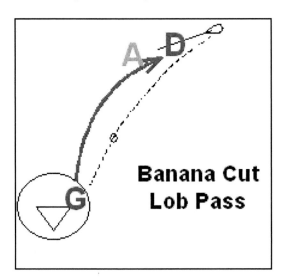

Practicing this regularly is vital to effective clearing, especially immediately after a save.

D. Catching

A good target help steammates throw where the keeper wants it

Catching a pass from a teammate is different than making a save, although the result is the same--gaining control of a bouncing ball or a ball in flight -- your team gets possession.

The setup is the same as throwing, turning the shoulders, hips and feet so that the are perpendicular to the line of flight of the ball. Then present a target to the thrower where the stick head is above the helmet as shown in the figure. With the stick a little ahead of the helmet, the keeper can see the ball into the stick and still have the hand position to give with the ball as it hits the stick. This produces very soft hands that can catch any pass of any speed.

Using this stance, the keeper can position his body between where he wants to catch the ball and the nearest riding offensive player and is already in the best throwing stance needed to move the ball effectively out of the defensive end.

Also, learn to catch "over the shoulder" so that the keeper can catch a throw even when being guarded. This takes practice but pays when helping on clears.

E. Ground Balls

A ground ball that the keeper gets is as good as a save.

Rake

The rake is used around the crease with the stick on top of the ball. By pulling the stick and the ball toward the keeper, the ball, when it comes out from under the stick it will spin into the stick, if not, it can be scooped. Care must be taken to not rake back toward the open goal, since over pulling may rake it into the net.

Goalie Rules

If the keeper has the ball under his stick in the crease and scoops it no one can interfere with the stick. Once in the stick, the stick cannot be checked (or it is an "interference" granting a free clear). If the ball is outside the crease and underneath the goalie stick the other team can attempt to dislodge it by running their stick under the goalie's stick. The keeper must hold the ball tightly to the ground and carefully pull it to the crease.

Open Field

In the open field, outside the crease, the rake is NOT recommended. Raking leaves too much time for the offensive team to make a run at the goalie. The preferred method is to do a running "scoop through" followed by an aggressive cradle up close to the helmet in preparation for a throw to a teammate. It is important to scoop with both hands preferably with the top hand close to the stick throat. By getting that hand and the back hand down the ball will go easily into the stick or be pushed forward for another try.

Cradle

Use a helmet level cradle by rolling the wrists and the fingers of the top hand to rotate the stick in an effective cradle. The best ground ball move is to cradle immediately after the scoop in one motion into a hip cradle and then transition to helmet level while running.

Turn to the Bottom Hand

As the ball is scooped, the keeper keeps running and turns in direction of the bottom hand. If one turns toward top hand side, the stick is exposed to a check from behind.

Do Drills

Since ground balls are free saves, have the keeper practice with the team on ground ball drills.

CHAPTER 3

Goal Play

Field Zones The field is broken down into zones from the goalie's point of view as shown below. The names are arranged in the terms as the goalie calls out the position of the ball to the defense during the game (see Goalie Talk below)

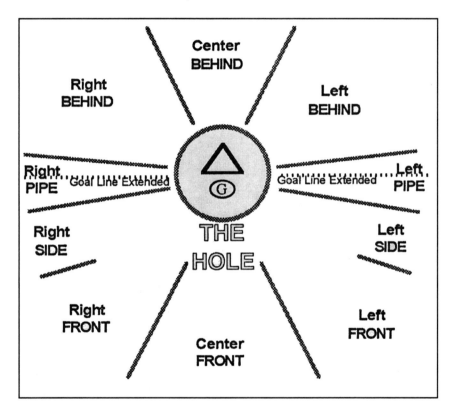

The field is divided into zones that the goalie uses to communicate to the defense where the ball is

A. Playing the Angles

Protect the Pipe The keeper should be between the ball and the goal, shading a bit to the near post (the post nearest the left elbow if the ball is LEFT FRONT or SIDE LEFT). With a even wider stance than shown, the keeper seems to cover more goal (discouraging the shooter and making it easier to step). This seems to expose the area between the feet, but that save has to be made anyway.

The goalie is between the ball and the goal.

Moving on an Arc As the ball moves (by passing or player movement), the keeper needs to reposition along an arc in front of the goal as shown in this figure.

The arc begins just outside one post and finishes just outside the other post. It is important to NOT go post to post. When the keeper's foot or leg hits the post, that side of the keeper's body tends to stiffen unconsciously leading to a straight or locked leg pipe side severely limiting the next move. This is called "getting your butt stuck in the goal", the keeper too far back and probably mentally backing up too - a mistake.

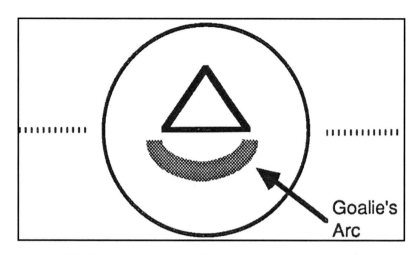

Moving along an arc positions to protect the goal

High Arc

Some keepers move along an arc farther from the goal line. It requires more frequent and quicker footwork to reposition optimally between shooter and goal.

Ladies Arc

A higher arc cuts down angle for the shooter to see an open spot to shoot at. A high arc makes the keeper more exposed to cross-crease pass (more steps to the far post). Many men keepers use a low arc for this reason. Women use a high arc since the cross-crease pass is harder with a women's stick allowing cutting off angle.

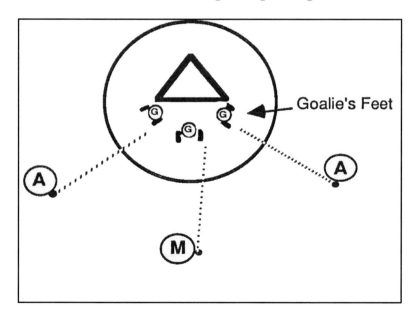

Arc play keeps the keeper facing the ball

The correct foot placement along the arc is shown in the figure below for three positions, Center Front, Side Left and Side Right.

Tapping the Pipe   The foot is not used to find where the keeper is in relation to the pipe. Other techniques are used. Looking at the pipe means looking away from the ball (bad move). By tapping the pipe with the head of the stick or the butt of the stick (depending on which side the keeper is on), the keeper can locate the pipe and determine his position without taking his eye off the play. But, this takes the top hand away from pointing at the ball. So use off-field landmarks to tell when you are close to the pipe.

Reference Points   Landmarks work for judging your position by using a reference point closer to the horizon. For centering, look at the opposite goal and then line up something farther away (say a fence post) with one of the goal posts when you are centered in the goal. When you need to re-center, just look for the fence post/goal pipe to line up. Similarly, pick out an object outside the field that is recognized when you are at the pipe (one for each side of the field). When you are facing it you are on that pipe.

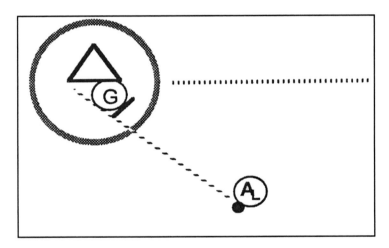

*Good body positioning discourages the shooter
from shooting at the near pipe*

**Forcing a
Perfect Shot**   Teaching the keeper good position involves having the keeper make the shooter make a "perfect shot" – the toughest shot possible to score. The lower the angle that the shooter has the better. From a position point of view, the most vulnerable spot (the area least covered by the goalie's position) should be the hardest possible shot for the shooter to execute. For example, when the shooter is on his right (the goalie's left) of the goal, the keeper wants the shooter to shoot at the far pipe. This is known as the LONG PIPE. It is harder to shoot at than the side closer to the shooter. Top corner LONG PIPE is easier to hit than bottom corner LONG PIPE. So good position tells us to hug ball-side PIPE with a wide stance and play the shooter more for a high shot than a low shot.

B. Playing Feed, Drives and Ball Behind

Beyond the basic positioning for where the ball is on the field, positioning and repositioning as the ball is passed or the shooter drives down the alley or across the face of the goal is critical to making saves. The keeper must learn to be effective even with all the distraction of repositioning and of the shooters/ball motion itself. There are some vital concepts involved;

Watch the ball using eyes and top hand as a pointer resetting stance/position based upon that siting pointing.Focusing on the ball in the stick, off the lip, in flight toward the goal and into the goalie's pocketminimizes the effect of the distraction of the running motion or shooting motion of the shooter. Similarly, the same technique applied to all passes, it not only minimizes the effect of the motions (distractions) involved but also allows the stance reset to be accomplished accurately and early (before the shot).

Ready – Getting into a productive stance before the shot improves the chance of making the save. A keeper whose feet are moving before the shot is not ready to step react to the shot and thus is limited by the extent of his concentration and hands only moves. When the ball is moving, the body moves well from a goalie point of view by setting up behind the top hand. This approach aids in keeping contact with the ball and in early cover of the top of the goal (the feed receiver will shoot high to high if there is space showing high).

Position - where and how the keeper moves effects the shooter and can be used to advantage. The shooters are taught to get the goalie moving and then shoot to where he/she moved from. For example, a shooter driving down the right hand alley is taught to shoot at the left pipe (right hand of the shooter). Since keeper basics indicate that the keeper should cover the pipe on that side of the field, that far pipe is probably more open. Some circumstances modify the basic "protect the pipe" to overcome the "long pipe" shooter is discussed below under Sweep shots

Behind Feeds When the ball is "BEHIND" the goal, the goalie places himself centered between the pipes and one or so yard from the goal line, FACING BEHIND, see figure. Thus, the goalie DOES NOT hug the pipe and peek around the goal at the feeder (peek around leaves no defense against the pass across the top of the goal to the opposite side). Perfect position allows the goalie to pivot in a single quick move on the ball side foot all the way around to face forward when the ball is feed to a player above GLE.

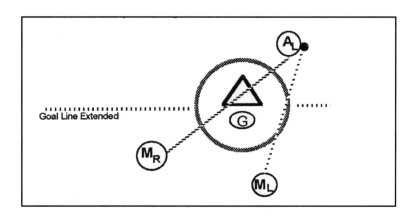

A centered goalie can pivot on feeds and
can catch some feeds, as if they were shots

Position for Full Coverage

When a behind attackman, A_L, passes over the top of the goal to middie, M_R, that pass can be protected from this position. If the pass goes through to middie M_R then there is time to PIVOT to the PIPE on that side already prepared to face a shot (by pointing at the passed ball with the top hand during the pivot turn).

If the pass goes to the M_L middie, it is usually unwise to attempt the pick-off of the pass (since this leaves the goalie out of position should he miss the pick-off). The goalie pivots on the pipe side foot to the post on the side where the pass is GOING, watching the ball in flight all the time (by pointing at it with the top hand), and STEPS toward where the ball is GOING to position for the save (stepping if the feed is not to a player right on the pipe)

Loop Passes

If the pass is looped over the goal from Center BEHIND to Center FRONT then the ball is <u>watched in flight</u> while the goalie turns around to face the potential shooter in front of the goal. A pick-off of this pass is possible, but, if the goalie has to jump to make the pick-off, then he should not and instead should concentrate on the flight of the ball and on turning to face the shooter.

Each of these from BEHIND feed scenarios should be practiced, daily. Part of warm-ups should include feeds from behind so that the keeper practices the pivot step to the post, watching the flight of the ball and the step to where the ball is GOING if a repositioning is needed.

Reacting to Behind Feeds

This emphasis on where the ball is going is lost on some players. As you practice reacting to behind feeds, the keeper will learn that the flight of the ball shows him where the ball will be caught. By pointing at the ball in flight and setting up behind that hand, the keeper will go to where the ball will land and sets up accordingly (and usually earlier than other approaches)

Eye-thumb-ball   Tracking the ball is vital. The idea is to be ready and in a productive stance by the time the ball is caught, with hands high and out front to react quickly to a shot off a feed. Experience with turns and setups after feeds teaches that using the eye-thumb-ball technique to track the ball's flight allows for the EARLIEST setup -- much earlier than if the eyes move and then the body. Wherever the hand goes, the body will follow (if the hand is up in the keepers line of sight). This is a powerful technique, possibly the best technique to provide the highest speed hand and body reaction to the ball.

Turns on Feeds   In addition to the techniques discussed in the next subsection on feeds and repositioning there are three key points critical to success of the turn during the back to front feed:

1) Turn staying on the balls of the feet so that the body can move with the hands to a quick shot.
2) Track the ball by pointing the top hand at the ball in flight during the feed (retaining concentration on the ball from the feeder and into the stick of the shooter).
3) Push the hands away from the chest to keep hands and elbows in front and weight forward to be ready for the shot just as the ball is caught by the shooter.

When a feed is made inside, there is little time for the keeper to waste. Roughly the shooter can shoot in a ¼ second, a keeper can save one in a ¼ second, so the keeper has a chance on inside feeds. But, if the keeper looses track of the ball, it takes about a ¼ second to reacquire the ball increasing the save time to ½ second or more. So watching the ball (with both the eyes and by pointing the top hand), keep the concentration on the ball. These are critical factors to keep the goalie able to make the save with the stick instead of just being a placard around which the shooter must shoot. A corollary to pointing and watching is to always face the ball and step forward (not backward) while moving.

Alley Drive Shots   – These shots are easiest of the movement oriented shot since the shooter stays on the same side of the field as he/she drives down the alley to shoot. The major problem for the keeper is focusing on the ball in the stick, off the lip of the stick, shot in flight and into the goalie stick pocket instead of being distracted by all the motions of the body, hands and legs of the shooter. In addition, the shooter is probably shooting the long pipe, since the keeper is covering the ball side pipe. None-the-less, this shot should be practiced to overcome the distraction of movement and to find a balance between protecting the pipe and still being able to over the "long pipe" shot.

Both sides need to be practiced since the shooting motion as seen by the keeper is different.

Sweep Drive Shots

A moving shooter, especially one that is sweeping across the face of the goal presents more complex distractions to the keeper because not only does the shooter have the opportunity to shoot all corners but the keeper needs to reposition as the shooter moves. The goalie's tendency is to stay squared up on the shooter and move to protect the ball side pipe, but this leaves the long pipe exposed as the shooter shoots where the keeper has just left (as he repositions). The best technique is to "trail the shooter" (move less quickly to the ball side pipe) by squaring up on the back hip of shooter (instead of the stick head). This delays the reposition to the ball side pipe and covers the "long pipe" either stifling the shot or making the shooter shoot the near pipe – very difficult to control on the move.

Cross Crease Feeds

The cross-crease feed is another complex situation since the keeper must also get cross crease In time to be in a effective ready stance to be involved in the save. This pass is a preferred part of efficient offenses and must be practiced. Best technique involves running from post to post behind the top hand that tracks the ball to its destination. Since the pass is an alternative to shooting, the keeper must focus on the initial shooter until the pass to another begins. By tracking the ball in the now passer's stick, off the lip, through the air and into the receiver's stick, the keeper can run to the other side while retaining eye and pointing contact with the ball.

The running steps tend to be different for each keeper and needs to be practiced until the keeper can get smoothly and quickly to the far pipe before the ball receiver shoots. Tracking the ball with the top hand is very effective and will yield saves as long as the keeper watches the ball equally intensely. Since the footwork is different right to left and left to right, both directions need practice. But, more feeds come from the right (facing the goal) than left (except on fast break) because there are more right handed finishers on teams than lefty finishers. Additionally, for a right handed goalie the turn for the right handed goalie from his left pipe to his right pipe is a hard turn (since the shoulders must be turned independently of the hand move). Thus, practice the left side to right side (goalie's view) pass more. The other direction is much easier. Use the passing and drive drills in the Drills section to teach your keeper these save situations.

Inside Moves/ Fakes

The better the shooter is the more he or she will fake to "freeze" the goalie or to "move" the goalie a little prior to the actual shot. The most effective of these is the ¼ turn fake, the dip & dunk, the dunk & dip and the ball hide behind the helmet. There are other fakes involved with dodges. The split dodge is the hardest dodge for the keeper since it interrupts the rhythm of the shooter in the goalie's view (the shooters body language) and introduces other rhythm/ motions inherent in having the stick in the other hand. Since it is the fastest of the dodges and effective inside too, this move and common fakes need to be practiced so that keeper can learn to ignore the distraction of the fake or dodge and focus on the ball – not the shooter. Many a keeper goes into "block mode" when the ball comes in close instead of tracking the ball with hands up and out in a productive stance. By using the Six Yard Drill (see Drills) and that drill with fakes and even split dodges, the keeper will gain confidence in their ability to make tough saves in close.

Hitting the Shooter

When the ball is fed in tight to the crease, there are opportunities to level the shooter by running into him just as the ball arrives from the feeder. Although this play is spectacular and effective for the original shooter, it usually leaves the keeper down and out of position to save any shots resulting from the loose ball involved with the hit. Only use this move when you have a clean shot at the shooter, otherwise, step out to cut down the angle and concentrate on moving the feet to reposition between him and the goal while covering his stick by pointing with the tops hand at the ball.

C. Playing the Shooter's Hands

Shooters' Hands

Some shooters give away what he is going to do by position of his hands and stick. The most dangerous shooter is one that holds his hands so that the stick is nearly vertical giving away the least by retaining the most options. The best technique that yields the most saves is to watch the ball a) in the stick, b) off the stick lip, c) throughout the whole shot flight and d) into the goalie stick pocket. But, every keeper gets some read from the shooter's motion, so watch the ball first but use the motion read some also.

Underhand Shooters

The shooter's hands are visible without losing sight of the ball. For example, there are very few shooters that drop their hands to the side (and the head of the stick below hip level) for what looks to be a low shot and have the ball rise as it goes toward the goal. Thus, one of the first rules of learning shooters is;

STICK HEAD LOW, GET DOWN (for a low shot)

Another way to say this is;

IF HE DROPS HIS HANDS, GET READY LOW

and, if he can do the riser, the keeper will see that by watching the ball tracking it to a high save. It is easier to rise with this shot than it is to go down (if you were planning on a riser and got fooled), so when in doubt get your butt low so that low is easy and high is too.

Sidearm Shooters

Likewise, if the shooter shoots sidearm, it is very difficult for him or her to 1) make a bounce shot or, 2) put the ball on the right pipe (the shooter's right for a right handed shooter). He's going to pull the shot to the goalie's right. The keeper gets to see the ball earlier on a sidearm or low to high shot than a more overhand shot. So, instead of the keeper being concerned about this shot, it is to the keeper's advantage for the shooter to shoot lo-lo, lo-hi or sidearm. Practicing saves on these shots will teach the keeper to be confident about them.

Dangerous Shooters

The dangerous shooter keeps the stick vertical until late in his motion and shoots overhand (or fakes an overhand shot before using another motion). This shooter can go left or right, up or down or pass. For this type of shooter, play the ball, not his head or eyes. As the game progresses the keeper needs to learn the shooter's tendencies and adjust. As he improves, it frustrates the shooter (to the keeper's advantage).

D. Talking to the Defense

People's Names

A goalie needs to know all of his teammates' names. To get their attention (to throw them a pass or to move them around defensively), the only sure thing that they know is their name. Besides being courteous, it works.

Talking to the defense from the goal raises the level of play of the defense. Letting them know where the ball is and what the status is very important. More vocal goalies get more out of their defense than quiet goalies. This is worth 3-5 goals a game. So it is not just a matter of style or personality, being vocal is a necessity.

Great Play

Every keeper at one time or another has been embarr-assed by a goal given up and may want to criticize a teammate for letting that player get in on the keeper. If the keeper criticizes the player, their relationship will get worse, not better. It is important to have the keeper understand that the rest of the defense keeps the ball off the keeper and even gets the ball back to our offense many times. When the defense breaks down, it is the keeper's turn to stop them from scoring. Any good play and especially one that gets the ball back (save, check, GB, run-out, etc.) should be cheered loudly by the keeper, "Great Play". And, if there is any other conversation, the most a goalie should say is "get the next one" showing confidence in his defense. The defense knows when the goalie let one in and in that situation one would hope that the defense would say "get the next one" to the keeper. If both encourage instead of criticize they all will play harder for each other.

Meaningful Calls The most critical calls change what the defense needs to do. They include "CHECK", "REBOUND", "CLEAR" and "SLIDE". Those need to be **shouted** and the others need to be at a lower level. Too much talking means the keeper will be ignored, so make these meaningful.

Ball Position The most practical way to be vocal is to call out where the ball is for the defense. Figure III-1 shows the common names for every area. When the ball moves, yell out the new position;

"BALL, CENTER FRONT"

"BALL, LEFT FRONT" or "LEFT FRONT"

as it is passed,

"BALL, LEFT BEHIND"

as the attackman come back to the pipe on the left side

"PIPE, LEFT PIPE"

Make sure that the call is made in a comfortable rhythm, that the defenders can hear and use to advantage.

Defensive Calls As play develops, defensive calls help the defense play better;

"CHECK" used when a feeder makes a pass to potential shooter. This alerts defenders to check sticks of the offensive players so that they cannot catch the feed.

"SLIDE" used when the on-ball defender is beat or needs help by having another defender slide to the ball carrier/shooter. Alternative calls include;

"BINGO!!" or "FIRE" or "GO" or "RED"

The word needs to be distinctive and short, one that a keeper can yell when he is under a lot of stress and one that everyone knows what it means when they hear it.

The whole defense needs to react by either moving to the shooter

(sliding) or covering a man that is uncovered because another
defender is sliding to the shooter.

"REBOUND" used to indicate the ball is still loose in front of the goal
– teammates knock down people on the crease and go for the
loose ball / start the clear.

"SHOOTER" used when the offensive man with the ball is preparing
to shoot. This alerts the defense to check him or to step in front
of the shot.

"HOLD" used to STOP the progress of the offensive player toward
the goal (nearly too close already).

"FEEDER" used when an offensive player, usually a behind attackman,
is set up to feed to cutting players. It alerts defenders to play their
men closely so that no good feed opportunity is given up.

"TOO FAR OUT" or **"DROP"** used when a defender is playing an
offensive player (usually with the ball) too far from the goal (and
thus is subject to being beat without help).

"HELP IN THE HOLE" or **"CRASH"** used during an unsettled situation
where there are uncovered offensive players near or approaching
the crease and the goalie needs some basic defensive help in the
hole.

"WHO'S HOT" used to get the defense to say who is the slide guy.

"WHO'S 2" is for the second slider.

Shots   When the shooter shoots, the team needs to know. By announcing,

"SHOT !!!"

two things happen:

1) The defender who is defending the shooter can step into the shot
to keep it from coming to the keeper.
2) The whole defense can prepare for either a clear or a loose ball if
there is a rebound.

A quiet goalie misses these opportunities.

Sprint after Shots If the shot misses the goal, the goalie must SPRINT after it. If he is
closest to the ball as it leaves the field of play, then the ball is awarded
to the keeper's team. If not, the other team remains on offense.

Thus, this sprint is as important as a save, since it gets the keeper's team the ball (and keeps it from the other team).

Save/Clears As the keeper makes the save or picks up a loose ball or rebound, he should announce;

"CLEAR !!"

telling the defense to start the clear.

The clear needs a quarterback and the goalie is in the best position to talk the team through it using terms like;

"ALL YOU" – tells the ball carrier to go up field with the ball

"REDIRECT" - indicates to pass it back to the GOALIE

"CROSS FIELD or SWING" – pass it to a defender at the other side of the field

"DIAGONAL" – pass it to a clearing player up field and cross field

"ONE MORE" – pass the ball straight up field Coaches need to have all the clearing players know what these mean and use them to effect the clear.

E. Post Save Keys

Defensive Helper As the clear begins, the men's keeper has 4 seconds to throw the ball or exit the crease. In order to have the MOST time, there should be a designated "outlet" defenseman who moves to a spot on the field usually on GLE at the box (men) when the goalie yells

"CLEAR!!"

If a pass isn't made up field to start the fast break then the goalie knows that he can pass to this "outlet" player.

Moving to the Back of the Goal

If there is no immediate pass up field, then the keeper should exit the crease, usually to the rear. Some keepers go immediately behind the goal and throw up field from there stepping out of the crease only as the 4 second rule time (or 10 seconds for women) expires.

Having the keeper stay in front of the cage allows the quickest available outlet pass. If defense breakout is slow forming, the keeper can pass to the "outlet" defenseman who can either throw the up field pass or return the ball the goalie as he exits the crease.

Most teams leave the goalie alone after he has made his first pass. If the defenders handle the ball well, then the keeper can break up field to help the clear. Many times, he will not be covered (since there is no one that naturally lines up with the keeper). If the keeper does not catch and throw well on the run, then spend time teaching him to do it to improve, you need that skill.

F. Defensive Help

Tending goal is easiest when the defense allows NO SHOTS. But, this is rarely the case. Teaching the defense to give up only the lower percentage shots is vital. As a goal tender, the keeper has the time to analyze what the offense is doing. Using this analysis to advise the coach or his teammates (if they are mature enough to listen) can be very important to adjusting the defense during the game.

The best defense gives up low angle shots from farther out than 12 yards while keeping the offense from screening the goalie's view of the ball or the play.

Outside Shots

Work with the defense to keep the shooter outside. If the defense can avoid being dodged and can cover the cutter, then the offense must shoot outside the perimeter of the defense. With the interior defense moving screens, the keeper has a long look at outside shots.

Low Angle

There are times when the offensive plays or players are so effective that they break through the perimeter and are shooting closer to the goal. The key is to lessen the angle - the lower the angle, the easier the save. If the shooter is 6 yards from the crease in the middle of the field, then he has more options than a goalie can cover.

Defense can improve the goalies chances if a) help (slides) comes from the hole at the shooter (the hole being the area directly in front of the goal) and b) the slide moves the shooter to one side or the other, denying the middle and **CUTS DOWN THE ANGLE.**

G. Fast Break Defense

There are five kinds of odd man defensive situations – defenses were there are fewer defenders than offensive players. For each there is an approach. One key consideration of team defense is that there is a goalkeeper and a crease to, both help the defensive player to minimize the impact of the offensive advantage. The five situations are:

Break 1 – only one defensive player back – drive the advancing middie or attackman down the alley (the side of the field he/she is on) and don't let him/her come across the face of the goal or back up top, once at GLE. If that player rolls under to the crease, push them, within the rules into the crease for the turnover. The low angle allows the goalie to help and the crease gives another defender.

Break 2 – two defenders back – they sit in a stack one in front of another in front of the goalie – the highest one takes the ball down the side and the other takes whomever is passed the ball. The 1st defender recovers to the front of the goalie and takes the next player that the ball is passed to, taking him/her down the side. In the women's game this stack is restricted by the 3 second rule, but the off-ball defender returns to a low defender position and slides to the next ball carrier as it is passed.

Break 3 – three defenders back – this is the most common defensive situation and is covered in more detail below.

Break 4 – four defenders back – set up a box with the farthest from the ball defending the middle of the box when needed

Break 5 – five defenders back – set up a box with a middle player (5 on a dice) and play zone until all even (men). For women the 3 second rule forces adjustment to a 3-2 set with 3 on the 8 meter and 2 outside the 8 next to the crease near the goal posts on either side. When an o-player enters the 8 from above, the weak side high player covers her first and from low on the side the low side defender moves first.

Goalie Helps   The goalie runs the break by alerting the defense of the situation by yelling **Break 1** or **2** or **3** or **4** or **5** indicating

Break-3 Defense is a Triangle of Three Defenders

how many defenders there are and what formation/ method to use to defend. The goalie also directs the defense play such as Hold to not rotate to the ball (let player move in or shoot) or to go to ball (Stop the Ball).

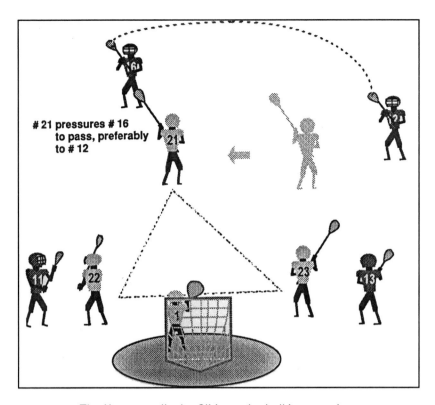

21 pressures # 16
to pass, preferably
to # 12

The Keeper calls the Slide as the ball is passed

Break-3 Basic Triangle

The Break-3 defense is an "extra man" situation for the offense where for a period of time, the offense has three attackmen and one or more middies to the defense's three defenders (and a goal keeper).

When a fast break develops, the basic formation is the triangle (see figure). The defensive team needs to know who is going to slide to the middie with the ball. This defensive person is called the "point man". Part of a goalie's directing the defense is to make sure that the close defense and keeper all know who the point man is.

As pressure is put on the incoming player with the ball, usually by a slide by the point man to the ball carrier, a pass will be attempted by that player to an open man. The defense is trying to have that person be the offensive player that is farthest from the goal.

As the pass is made, each defender moves into a new position in a sliding zone as shown in the figures The purpose of all of this is to either give up an outside shot (that the goalie should handle) or buy time until the defensive middies arrive to even up the teams.

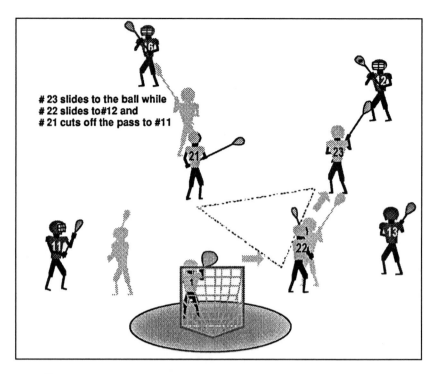

23 slides to the ball while
22 slides to#12 and
21 cuts off the pass to #11

The defense moves to defend the ball and the passing lanes
(keeping their triangle alignment throughout)

Slide Call

First, goalie tells the defense about the fast break;

"FAST BREAK" or "BREAK 3"

Second, the goalie calls the slides that occur simultan-eously as the ball is passed from the breaking middie to the point attackman (and again on each pass) by yelling;

"SLIDE"

helping the team move as one defensively.

Save or Hit

During a fast break it is tempting for the keeper to move from the goal to hit the offensive player closest to the crease (as he is shooting). If the hit can be done as he is catching a pass it may work. If the hit is attempted after the pass is caught it usually results in a score.

Most coaches would rather have the keeper stay in the goal ready to make the save than the make the hit. As a keeper, I love the hit that gets the attackman just as he is trying to catch the ball. This is a BIG play for a keeper so let him go once in a while.

H. Clears

Once the ball is saved, or when the defense gains control of the ball in the defensive end, the goalie, defense and middies need to CLEAR the ball across midfield. The "quarterback" of the clear is the keeper, so he needs to know all the plays that produce CLEARS. Coaches need to teach this to keepers the clears so that they can help the team clear (instead of see the clear break down usually with bad results).

The goalie is critical to the clear because of the nature of the rules of the game. Normally the riding team has three attackmen and three middies riding against three defenseman and three middies (with the riding defensemen covering the clearing attackmen on the other half of the field).

An effective clearing goalie produces a one man advantage to the clearing team over the riding team in the defensive half of the field. If the keeper is not active in the clear or is ineffective at handling and moving the ball, then this advantage is lost, making the clear difficult.

One of the goals each goalkeeper should have for any game is to start his team's fast break (either by an effective outlet pass off the save or through an effective clearing play).

Outlet Pass - Big Play
The outlet pass is really a team play. It begins with the save and the setting up of a defensive helper for the keeper (usually at GLE and the box line on the goalie's stick side). This helper allows the keeper maximum time to throw a pass before exiting the crease before the 4 second (men) or 10 second (women) time expires. And/or he throws to the helper who can also throw the outlet pass.

Starting the Clear
The figure shows the normal defensive set (no offensive players shown). When the goalie yells,

"CLEAR!!"

the defenders and middies move to positions that:

1) Make it hard for the opposition to cover them
2) Get them into positions up field where the keeper can hit them with a pass – like the banana cut outlet pass.
3) Provide an outlet for the keeper in case an up field pass does not develop.

The figure shows the breakout of all the defenders and middies and one of the possible passes.

*As the save is made the whole defense moves to new
positions to start the clear*

Take Three Looks The keeper has a chance, if his team breaks up field, to immediately
throw an outlet pass. Some keepers are more worried about the 4
second rule than the pass. To teach them a good rhythm, use the
three looks approach;

Look One - After the save, look to the left top corner of the box, if
the player is open pass it to them (this is the best pass since most
players catch right handed and the pass is thrown to lead the
player with a right handed catch).

Look Two - If there is no one open to the left, look straight up the
field. If the player is open, pass it to him. It is better to lob it
almost over their heads and let them run it down than to try to
pass it through someone (especially in this the most vulnerable
middle of the field).

Look Three - If there is an open player at the right top corner of the
box, pass it to him (or her). Otherwise, pass it to the defensive
helper on your right, who by this time should be yelling, your
name or;

"Here's Your Help!!"

If the keeper does not hear this call on the third count then he
should exit the back of the crease and prepare for a slower clear.

Three looks take less than a second a piece leaving a full second to exit if needed (boys).

Women too

For girls, the keeper should still take three looks, but should take two seconds for each one, letting the play develop a bit. This uses more of the 10 seconds allotted and still leaves time to pass to the outlet helper defender.

Set Clears

The set clear has two objectives;

1) Get the ball cleared over the mid-line to the offense
2) Set up a two-on-one to do it.

Setting up the two-on-one is done not just because the clearing team has an extra man, but because the imbalance can turn into a similar overload at the offensive end (resulting in a goal). The better the clearing team runs the two-on-one situations, the more often it results in defensive slides in the offensive end that can mean a goal.

Drive Up Field

The goal keeper is key since he can look for and find where the right pass yields a two-on-one. If a pass does not yield a two-on-one then the keeper is the one who is open (un-pressured). In this circumstance the keeper needs to drive the ball up field to one side until either some riding player slides to him or he goes over the mid-line. If someone slides to the keeper, it is very likely that the clearing player in the area that the slider came from is open (if not, swing / pass the ball to the opposite side of the field). For women, it is unwise for the keeper to advance the ball beyond the defensive 30 yard line since a stoppage of play can leave the goal unguarded.

Cross the Mid-line

If no one slides to the keeper he should go into the offensive zone. It is critical that in that area (where the sides are even) that the offensive team provide him an outlet (someone to pass to). Most teams cover the goalie almost immediately after he crosses the mid-line and try to cover tightly anyone who is close by.

Pass to the Attack

Clearing teams should set up a pick for an attackman (by a middie) at the corner of the box. The attackman uses to get free of the defenseman for a pass from the keeper.

If there is no one to pass to at this point, the keeper can throw the ball into the deepest offensive corner, where the attack can run down the ground ball.

Four Across clear is used with good stick handling defensemen

Four Set Clears   If the defense puts the ball into play from a whistle, there are four basic formations (Set Clears) used to spread out the riding players so that a two-on-one can be developed;

1) **Four Across** 1st figure - Not used much anymore
2) **3 Across or L Clear** next figure - Similar to Umbrella
3) **Umbrella Clear** next figure - Very Flexible
4) **Man Down Clear** - Special Clear

Four Across can be slow   The Four Across is used to develop a four-on-three (three defensemen and a goalie versus three attackmen) when the riding team rides the clearing middies man-to-man. The goalie walks the ball up the field until jumped by an attackman developing a two-on-one(either with him and the defenseman on his right--throw to him--or with the two defenseman on his left--throw to the open one).

The NCAA and high schools have adopted rules to speed up play, especially clearing. This clear is generally too slow developing under this rule (since it waits for the attack to jump the ball).

Spread the Field   Both the L and the Umbrella clears are Three Across clears (one goalie and two defensemen). This spreads out both the clearing team and the attack covering them. If the up field defenseman is not covered by an attack-man then that is the pass to make. If he is covered by an attackman then there are only two attackman to cover the goalie and the two defensemen.

By passing from the keeper to one side, either a two-on-one develops immediately or a second, cross-field pass to the opposite side defenseman produces a two-on-one.

L Clear

After these initial moves the two middies in the middle of the field break in opposite directions. If they are both covered, the two-on-one can continue up field across the mid-line (with the far side middie staying on-side).

3 Across or L puts one defensemen up at the substitution box and spreads the attack more

If one of the riding middies in the stack slides to the two-on-one then the clearing player passes to the now uncovered middie and the clearing team is on offense.

The L clear does well when it is operated the same as the Umbrella clear discussed in detail below.

Umbrella Clear

With NCAA clearing rules, the Umbrella Clear formation is used to spread out the riding team so that one mid-line area players can break to the goalie/defenseman who has the ball to receive a pass curl and make another pass. Since this breaking middie may be jumped by the riding team, he must have a pre-defined outlet pass (or 2) in mind to keep the ball moving faster than the slides of the riding team.

Thus, with umbrella clear, the clearing team passes from goalie to defenseman to breaking middie to middie outlet and the ball is cleared and many time results in a fast break for the clearing team.

The Umbrella clear is a modified L Clear used to clear the ball under the 20 second clearing rule

Invert the Umbrella

You can change the umbrella to two middies just outside restraining line and the two wing players almost up at the mid-line. This is very helpful in keeping the passes short. Should the riding team jump everyone except the defender farthest from the ball, have that player sprint into the box and on toward the ball handler and he will be open to receive the pass and turn up field with a two-on-one with the closest clearing middie.

Initial Pass

If the initial pass (goalie to wing defenseman) does not draw an attackman then the two-on-one approach up the side is used instead of the fast pass approach and the ball is cleared that way. This formation is the dominant formation in use in college and professional lacrosse. The usual play is to break both of the middies in the middle to the box, one will be open. Important variations are discussed below:

Tight Ride   If the ride is riding tight (attack on goalie and 2 defense-men, middies on 3 of the ball side middies/long stick nearer the midline) then the back side middie (farthest from the ball) breaks to the corner of the box, across and into the box to receive a pass. He then curls up field as the other middies drive up field for a 3-on-2 (usually).

Ten Man Ride   If the riding team is using a ten man ride then move all the players who are shown close to the midline 10 yards closer to the box. Then, no <u>riding</u> defenseman can cover a clearing middie (since the riding defenseman cannot cross the mid-line). This is vital. The team does not change it's plan/formation on a 10 man ride (with the riding goalie riding an attackman), it moves the mid-line players closer to the box and the 10 man breaks down.

Sagging Ride   If the riding team sags, letting the clearing team out of the box, an attackman will eventually jump the goalie who throws to the man that became uncovered (usually immediately in back of the jumping attackman or a wing defenseman) and a 2-1 begins as that middie curls and crosses the midline.

Watch the Trap   Many teams trap the ball carrier after he crosses the midline by cutting off the pass to that side attackman, sliding a defenseman to the ball and covering the middie at the midline with a riding middie (the third middie goes to the hole to cover the uncovered attackman). To do this the far side (back side) middie is left uncovered. The ball handling middie may need to pass a cross-field pass to this uncovered player to complete the clear.

Against Zone   Against a Zone Ride, the riding team almost always:

- Lets the goalie clear the ball outside the box
- Has the two point attackmen slide to the ball and to adjacent (the ball side players)
- The third attackman (at the mid-line in the middle with two middies, one on each side of the field) slides to the open long stick on the back side (opposite side of the field) as the clearing team passes to him.
- Ball side outside middie cuts off his man from the ball.

Since the riding team is using a 2-3 and 2-3 and the clearing team is using a 3-4-3, the clearing team has the riding team outnumbered in the area between the box and the midline. By using the middle two middies first, the goalie can open up the zone easily. If not, pass to the backside long stick and he has at least a 2 on 1 to clear the ball.

Attack Over

If all this doesn't work against a zone, have a middie step on the offensive end (as a defenseman steps off) against this soft zone and let an attackmen drive across the midline to the ball for a pass. He then curls back and makes the pass to the open middie (usually the one at the box) and a fast break starts.

Swing the Ball

If the riding team does slide well against the first or even the second pass, the clearing team keeper needs to stay alert to move the ball to someone is open on the other side of the field for a two-on-one and the ball is cleared. The keeper is vital here. The ball can come back to the keeper and he can pass it to the opposite side of the field ("swing" the ball to the opposite side) also.

The keeper needs to be in an outlet position after he passes (assuming that the riding team will slide well) and he needs to be prepared (by seeing who is where) to "swing" the ball to the opposite side. This means NOT in front of the goal (most defenders will not throw back to the keeper who is in front of the goal where a bad pass or catch could result in a goal). Remember that the clearing team has an extra man and finding the open person and getting them the ball is critical to clearing effectively.

Middie Down Clear

Some teams don't have good ball handling defensemen. In this case, the clearing team may use a specialized clear. One of these is the Middie Down clear, where a middie gets the ball before the whistle is blown and dodges his way to the mid-line. This is sometimes necessary, but the other members of the team should help by getting themselves open for outlet passes as the middie progresses. This makes the riding team stay honest even against a weaker ball handling defense.

Man Down Clear

When a team is man down and gets the ball on the end line during a dead ball situation, usually the offensive team will double team the ball with a bad result (loss of ball) because there is no one to throw to.

A set man down clear helps this situation. First, place the short stick defender in the crease at the back of the crease (as the goalie). Put the goalie on the back side corner (the man with the ball is on the ball side of the field). Put one long stick on the back side of the field at the midline. Bring an attackman to the midline (this should be a middie playing attack) and place the other long stick close to the box (ready for a middie sub). This spreads the riding team.

The back side long stick steps across the midline and the attackman breaks to the ball. If the attackman playing the short stick middie in the crease plays between the ball and the crease then this middie breaks up field, receives the pass, passes to the attackman and he and the middie stepping on (defenseman off) start up field to play keep away until the penalty is over.

If the short stick middie in the crease is played by the attackman in front of the cage, the ball is passed or rolled to him in the crease and he passes to the attackman coming in across the mid-line.

Stay Involved Keepers must remember that it is they that provide the extra man while clearing. So, after the initial pass, the keeper needs to stay in the play proving a "swing" if the ride is good or an outlet for anyone in the defensive end until the ball is in the offensive end.

Clearing Summary Clearing is another time when the goalie is the leader. He needs to not only know his role but everyone else's so that he can lead the team with the best pass and best setup of the clear. It is vital to teach the goalie to draw a man (when he is supposed to), make a crisp pass, stay active as an outlet should the ride turn back the clear to him, swing the ball (reverse it) effectively to re-energize the clear and otherwise make good, out of the goal clearing decisions for the team.

CHAPTER 4
EQUIPMENT

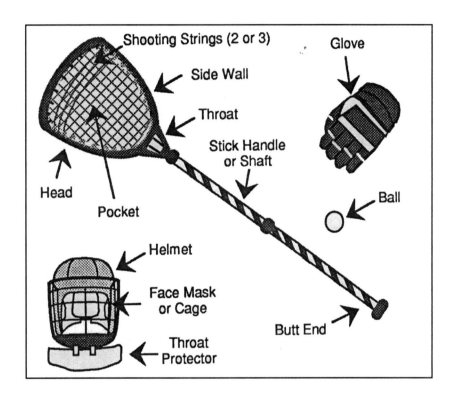

A. Lacrosse Stick

Stick   The goalie stick is the most important part of the goalie's equipment. For high school and beyond, we encourage keepers to not shorten the shaft. That shaft provides some counter balance to the weight of the head of the stick that allows the stick to rotate easier and faster (in a propeller motion). Some keepers (including myself) put an extra weight in the end of the stick (tape) for a more balanced stick for easier rotation.

Stick Length   The stick with a standard men's shaft from the manufacturer is just long enough to come up to the top of the shoulder of a 6 foot tall keeper. For a shorter keeper, the stick should come up to just under the chin. If it is much longer than that, the butt end will occasionally drag the ground at the wrong time.

For women the stick can be no longer than 48 inches. Rebalance the stick using tape on the butt end.

Pocket

A very few keepers play with a big stick pocket, sometimes called a "bag" to help in catching hard shots or in yielding fewer bounce shot rebounds. Too big a bag makes it very difficult to throw effectively. Too tight a pocket makes it hard to control the ball during the save or when throwing.

The pocket needs to be about 3-5 inches wide and deeper than the rest of the stick up close to the shooting string. When throwing, this is where the ball should be to have consistent throws. It the pocket (deepest part of the stick) is closer to the throat of the stick then it is difficult to throw the ball hard (or far).

Mesh

Most goalies use a mesh face instead of traditional (leather and string) stringing. The mesh is light, breaks in right away and can be easily adjusted as the stick wears.

Stringing

Two things are important about the goalie stick;

1) the way it was strung by the manufacturer or your local sports supplier is usually NOT good for playing
2) over time, the stringing/mesh will stretch or loosen or if left without playing regularly, it will shrink.

Thus, it is very important to learn (from an experienced goalkeeper or by trial and error) how the stick should be strung/feel and how to adjust the stringing by; tightening throwing strings, shortening the bag, or, as we do, use a river rock to periodically pound out the pocket.

B. Helmet and Pads

Helmet   The standard NOSCSAE approved helmet is required equipment. It
contains a four point chin strap hooked at all times to protect against
a rocking helmet that can injury the keeper during a shot. The current
generation of helmets is excellent, capable of stopping a shot from
the front easily without injury.

Added to the helmet is a bib or throat protector that protects the
throat from shots. There are different versions of throat protectors,
soft plastic and hard plastics. Both work effectively.

Mouth Guards   Mouth guards are required equipment in most youth and high school
leagues. Since goalies need to talk loudly during the game, he needs
to practice talking loudly (isn't that an unusual request for a coach
or teacher) with the mouth guard in. To facilitate this, the last third
of the mouth guard on each side can be cut off freeing the tongue
somewhat for speaking.

Chest Protector   Underneath the jersey, the keeper wears a chest protector that
protects the sternum portion of the chest and stops some bruises on
shots that are stopped by the trunk of the body. The best protectors
are narrow between the arms so as to not interfere during saves.

Shoulder &   Some youth leagues require every player to play with shoulder pads
Elbow Pads   and elbow pads. In high school and college, this equipment is usually
shed because it gets in the way of arm movements that are critical to
good reactions (and, of course, saves).

Once outside the goal, keepers benefit from elbow to protect from
checks while clearing the ball.

Shorts or Sweats Many keepers play in shorts, weather permitting. Others prefer
sweats. Sweat pants hide the bruises that keepers sometimes live with
and provide a low level of protection from shots. If the keeper is
nursing an injury, wears a knee or ankle brace or uses shin guards,
then sweats hide this equipment.

Cup   A cup should be worn by all lacrosse players. But, for keepers it is
vital. A cup save is a save, but it isn't clear if a keeper can remember a
save in the cup area if he isn't wearing a cup. The football style cup is
better than no cup, but is inferior to either the Bike brand "banana"
cup (pointed on one end) or the goalies girdle cup.

Shin Guards   At the youth and beginning levels, keepers should be encouraged
to use a good pair of soccer shin guards (ones with hard plastic,

one piece inserts). They save a lot of bruises and let the keeper gain needed confidence.

If a keeper gets shin splints or a deep leg bruise, using shin guards can making playing reasonable.

Women keepers sometimes wear large leg pads. They are legal and I don't recommend them. They tend to imply that the keeper should BLOCK the shot instead of save it with the stick. Indoor lacrosse goalies make saves with their pads, but outdoor men and women make most of their saves with the stick.

Gloves   Goalie gloves are superior to regular men's gloves since they have additional thumb protection and some finger and back of the hand protection. Goalie gloves are really mandatory especially at the higher level of scholastic and all college play.

C. Shoes

Wet Weather   Two types of shoes are needed for goaltending. One pair for hard ground and one for soft ground or wet (rain) conditions. If the crease is wet/muddy the shoe needs to have as deep a cleat as the league allows so that the most traction can be gained by the keeper. The Adidas or Nike soccer shoe with 4-5 screw in spikes (long) under the ball of the foot and two in the rear give great traction and are nearly self cleaning in muddy conditions.

Hard Ground   A lot of shoes work fine on hard ground. But, the cleated shoes mentioned above do not. I strongly suggest a 12 - 15 cleat soccer shoe. This shoe should not have a single cleat at the toe. Two front cleats lets the keeper move easier on the first step without catching the toe cleat.

Soccer shoes encourage the player to stand on the balls of the feet and should be used.

When playing on artificial turf, a turf shoe should be used. Some of these do not provide good 1st step traction. A very aggressive tread running shoe can work very well on turf. Some amount of protection for the toes is helpful (extra rubber that is higher than running shoes).

D. Ladies Equipment

Ladies Equipment The ladies equipment is very similar to the boys, except for the obvious groin protection changes (use goalie pants with protection). Shin guards are common. Some lady keepers have gravitated to heavy padding (bulky shin pads and padded arm pads). This fosters a blocking-of-the-shot style of play, actually inappropriate for today's goalies.

Chapter 5
Drills and Conditioning

Fatigue Makes Cowards of Us All

- Vince Lombardi

A. Drills

Repetitions

Coaching a lacrosse team is demanding. In order to have the team progress, the coach needs to spend some of each practice teaching or re-enforcing individual skills (after all it is an individual sport) and team skills (after all it is a team sport). This can be done in team activities (line drills, fast break drills, etc.), except for the keepers. Most team drills where keepers are in the goal simulate game conditions (good) that expect the keeper to perform at game level. This is helpful but does not provide a learning/ improvement environment.

Keepers need a lot of controlled repetitions to learn and improve. Some of these can be gained by teaching the keeper individual drills that re-enforce good technique. Any lacrosse player must be taught that, just like basketball, the player is going to improve by practicing on his or her own as much any other activity. Coaches need to emphasize it continually so that keepers will practice away from the team practices including catching and throwing, the walk-the-line drill, ball-toss drill and working on the wall on both throwing long and short and in playing goal on throws off the wall

Catching & Throwing

Coach Glen Theil, Head Lacrosse Coach at Penn State University, starts his goalie clinic by telling the keepers the first thing to learn is to handle the ball well, so he lines them up and teaches them to catch and throw. Goalies can do this in their back yard with a friend.

The key to getting something out of catching and throwing is to throw accurate, hard passes that hit the receiver in a 1 foot square area 1-foot to the side of his head. The keeper's feet should be turned as discussed in Chapter II on Throwing. Catching can be practiced as shown under Catching (Chapter II) or by simulating the save by using the goalie's best stance and save techniques. It is most important to practice making the save and then changing the stance to a throwing stance prior to cutting the pass loose.

The Wall

If there is no one to throw with, go to a good wall and throw and catch with it. This practice produces good throws and arm strength as well as ball concentration. As the keeper advances, he can throw hard, set up for the save, make the save and then throw again. This activity really helps in many skill areas.

Wall Throwing

For throwing get 10-12 balls and get 30 yards (younger players) or 40-50 yards from the wall and throw to hit the same spot about 7 feet high on the wall. The ball should come all the way back and the goalie can practice scooping ground balls. Practicing this with the left hand too, for a right handed goalie, helps the goalie develop into the best ball handler on the team.

Wall Saving

Use the wall to work on eye-hand coordination and reaction. My favorite drill is to use an attack stick and a wall. Throw the ball hard against the wall from 12 yards hi to hi setting up in your goalie stance while the ball is in flight and then make the save. Do 10 of these and step in one long stride and do it again. Keep throwing hard. Then step in again and do 10 more (if you drop the ball start over on that 10). Then step in again and do 10 more. Then step in and do 20 more. Then step in and do 20 more. Continue stepping in until you are 2-3 yards from the wall and can do 20 without dropping one. Then start again back at 12 yards and go hi to off side high and go through the sequence again. Then try high to hip and high to bounce saves off the wall. It will surprise you how much concentration on the ball and how much speed improvement you will gain.

Walking the Line

There is a drill that teaches the brain/muscles what to do on saves called "walking-the-line". It is accomplished by finding a line on the ground (like the sideline of a field), get into the save stance and choose a shot to simulate (say, off-side high). Visualize the shot in the mind, step to that save and move the stick, hands and body to make the simulated save. Then step back to the line, pick another shot type and make the move again and again until the move is fluid to all areas with a good step, good stick motion, good hand motion, good balance, etc.

This drill is repetitions at their best and helps the keeper understand how to make the moves without the pressure of having the ball coming at him at the same time.

This drill can be run with the coach and the keeper until the keeper both understands and executes the move to the ball. Then the keeper can practice these moves on his own to improve or to correct something in his mechanics

Ball Toss Drill

The ball is saved by the action of the top hand driving the stick head to the ball and the feet driving the body to help the hands get to the ball quicker. Ball toss is done without the stick and uses the gloved top hand to catch the ball while working on stepping and ball watching with the top hand leading to the ball. The goalie sets up in his/her best stance without a stick and a coach or another player tosses the ball overhand from about 3 yards away at the place where stick side high would be. The receiving goalie needs to:

a) catch the ball with thumb and forefinger
b) needs to step to the ball (from ball of foot to ball of foot – by pushing with the off-ball foot)

Then they reverse roles and the receiving goalie throws to the other goalie. They must get 10 in a row without dropping it once. If they drop the ball, then they start the count over. This is done a total of 8 times as follows:

1.) 10 IN A ROW to stick side high
2.) 10 to off stick side high
3.) 10 to stick side hip
4.) 10 to off stick side hip
5.) 10 to stick side low (shoe lace level)
6.) 10 to off stick side low (shoe lace level)
7.) 6 off the short bounce just outside of and in front of the foot on stick side
8.) 6 off the short bounce just outside of and in front of the foot on off stick side

If the keeper is stepping and watching the ball throughout the catch is easily learned. Don't let anyone catch in the palm and make them turn their wrists in the same rotation as must be used to guide the stick to the ball..

Tennis Ball Toss Drill

Laying on your back (usually indoors) and using a tennis ball, throw the ball in the air with the left hand (for right handed goalies) and catch the ball with the right hand. Each time start with the right hand in the save position (in front of the face to the right of the right eye) and track the ball with the top hand. This simple drill helps improve eye hand coordination and ball watching.

Coach's Time

Keepers can do a few things for themselves but a cap-able shooting coach is vital to a keeper's progress. A keeper needs to confront the natural human tendency to be passive or defensive when confronted with other humans charging toward you or throwing objects at you.

Watch, Ready, Go, Next

Sessions with the goalie are meant to build consistent high level of being **ready, watch-the-ball** and **go to the shot** when making the save when the keeper is later in a scrimmage or game. Next is getting mentally and physically ready for the next shot. These are the critical things that the keeper can control and need to be worked on continuously to ensure a high level of play.

Step-Over-The-Rope Drill

Many goalies try to make saves mostly with their hands and minimal stepping or stepping only laterally. This is too passive for the keeper and leads to misses that shouldn't be goals. The idea is to instill stepping TOWARD THE SHOT to move the hips to get the hands to the ball quicker. This is not an automatic action when being shot at. Drills from Mac Diange, Assistant Coach at Army help develop "Go" stepping. While the goalie is doing regular shooting, put a rope on the ground (or tape on artificial turf)) that parallels the goal line but is just in front of the goalies toes. Encourage the goalie to step over the rope on each shot and after most shots look and see if they did. They will begin to know when they took an aggressive step instead of a lateral or no step.

From-One-Side Drill

Great goalies make them in all corners of the goal easily by driving the top hand to the ball and stepping simultaneously with the ball side foot (using the triple step technique moving the hips and the hands to ball quicker.) A drill to work on this is to setup to one side of the goal and have the shooter shoot the ball right down the middle (or a little closer to the far pipe). To get to this shot the goalie must step and drive the hands at the same time. Since the goalie knows where the ball is going, this drill really helps them work on technique and timing. If they are cheating early to that side make them switch sides every 5 shots and they will learn this even better.- another great drill from Max Diange at Army

Six Yard Drill

The 6 yard drills and drive drills are used to teach the keeper to watch–the-ball (and not read the player). At the beginning, tell the keeper where you are going to shoot and then shoot there. He/she may be upset by how many go in. Work with them on watching the ball effectively and their aggressive stance that allows them to go to the ball on each shot. Coach's patience and encouragement will bring good results, eventually.

Feed Drills

Work on turns, footwork, ball tracking with the top and hand and staying in the shot until the end.

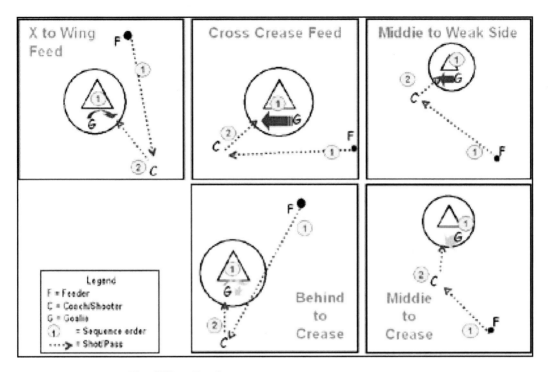

X to Wing Feed – This drill is tough since the keeper will tend to drop his/her hand during the feed/turn. This is fatal since reestablishing eye-hand-ball coordination takes longer than if it is just maintained. Work on keeping the top hand high, point it to the ball and focusing on the ball, the saves will come. Think about the "step to pipe, step to ball" turn, it works.

Cross-Crease Feed - For cross crease, the pipe side foot needs to be pointed toward the midline. Then when the other foot is lifted the pipe side foot can push and start the running sequence toward the other pipe. Some keepers use 3 steps, others 4, so work that out with the keeper. I use 3 in one direction and 4 in the other, but either case run past the pipe and setup so that it is harder for the shooter to shoot round the keeper.

Weak Side Feed - The Middie to weak side needs practice because most goaltenders drop their hands again on this pass instead of holding them high (and taking something away from the shooter), Again practice right to left and left to right.

Behind Wide to Crease - Behind to crease or Middie to crease should be done last in your progression since they are the hardest. Any drop in hands or weight on the heels, or stiff legs will usually mean a goal.

Don't do a lot of repetitions on these crease ones, but I do work with the keeper until he/she is in good form and getting some saves. If they get real frustrated on the crease ones then back off and work on the other feeds and put it back on your schedule for later after the keeper's overall feed tracking technique has improved.

Drive Drills   Drive drills help develop skill against moving shooters.

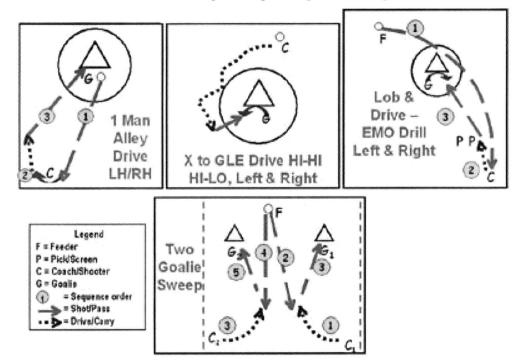

One Man Drive Drill – Out Front – In the 1 man drill the keeper throws to the middie/coach whose back is to the goal. He catches the ball over the shoulder and turns to the outside and drives down the alley taking a shot 10 yards from the keeper—high initially and later low. This drill provides a lots of distractions on the keeper, the catch, the turn, the ball being hidden by the turning shooter's body, the running and the shot motion on the move. It is very game like and helps the keeper get better.

Behind Drives - The X to GLE drive is an attack dodge and helps the keeper get used to all the tension and ball hiding that goes on at GLE. Do both left side and right side. Another form is to dodge from GLE and roll under GLE and back in front. Great competitive drill – shooter vs. keeper.

Sweep Drives - Although modern defenses aren't supposed to give up sweeps up top, sometimes they do and the keeper needs to practice them. We use two goals, two keepers, one feeder and two shooters alternating the sweep & feed shot sequence, all on the run. Two shooters and two keepers keeps thing moving without tiring out the shooters.

Lob and Drive - The Lob and Drive drill simulates the Extra man lob pass with a double pick. The keeper has to track the ball in the air where it lands behind a screen. The shooter drives to the pick and shoots just as he goes by the double pick. Very realistic drill.. Mix in some outside heat too, very game like – especially since this is the goal of some extra man plays

Outlets

Add outlets the keeper makes after the save. He/she throws a good outlet pass to one player usually outside the box who throws to one of the feeders who then throws to the shooter who continues the warm-up with what ever shot sequence he is working on.

Workouts

This means setting aside time, usually 30 minutes prior to practice start that is dedicated to the keeper. These are nearly as important as the game experience needed for the keeper to manage the pressures of the game.

Most of the repetitions the keeper requires need to be in the cage where a shooter is providing specific shot sequences and feedback that the goalie can learn from. Most drills are focused as building blocks toward a consistent high performance. One area includes shot sequences to accomplish this including:

- High-to-high from 12-14 yards
- Low-to-low from 10-12 yards
- High to low from 10-12 yards
- High-to-high and high-to-low off cross-crease feeds
- High to high off rear to front feeds
- High-to-high from 5-6 yards
- High-to-high from 5-6 yards with fakes
- High-to-low from 5-6 yards with fakes
- Drive shots from out front down the alley (both sides)
- Drive shots with split dodge or roll dodge out front
- Drive shots from behind, low angle and roll back

B. Warm-Ups

Warm-ups

The purpose of the warm-up is different in practice than before a game. Before a game, the key is to move the keeper through the warm-up stages:

Seeing the ball and stepping – shooting high to high, pick up the speed of the shot early so that the keeper watches the ball at near game speeds while working on stepping.

Reacting to the shot - Work on each area in sequence (stick side high, off-side high, stick side hip, off-side hip, low shots stick side (no bounce--worm burners), low shots off side (worm burners)

Attacking the Shot and Making the save - Use overhand bounce shots that require a strong step to the ball (attacking) then mix in other shots to all areas. Pick up shot speed to the highest level. Sometimes use a screening offensive player to practice screen saves.

Moving with the play - Use one person behind and one in front opposite the shooter; pass the ball before shooting having the keeper move with the passes.

Talking - Call the ball position and the shot just like talking to/with the defense during the game.

During each stage it is important to continually move in an arc in front of the goal 12-15 yards out from the keeper (until the feeding stage where closer shots are used too).

Basics

Warm-ups are a progression of more difficult activities that move the goalie from not seeing and slow reaction to almost tunnel vision and smooth quick reactions. There are stages to the warm-up. A good sequence is:

Pops - Working within 2 yards of the crease, throw the ball at the goalies stick side and get a return. Work quick pops in an arc across the front of the cage. This is one of the best drills to get the keeper watching only the ball.

Outside High Shots - Moving out to 12-14 yards and walking in an arc from post to post in front of the goal, shoot 10-15 shots to stick side high. Use shots with good speed since this is when he gets used to the ball coming in on him. Encourage him to make a step to the ball on these saves with the stick side foot. Take a break (about a two count or one strong look away) between each shot to allow the keeper to reset.

Continue to walk the arc back and forth now shooting 10-15 shots to the off-side high area. Use fast shots, check hand position for good rotation and encourage a strong step with the off side foot.

Repeat this for the stick side hip and off side hip.

Worm Burners - Working on the same arc 12-14 yards out, shoot shots that go right along the ground (no appreciable bounce). Work stick side low, then 5 hole then off side low with 10-15 shots each. Encourage the step, "butt down", good hand height (eye-thumb-ball) and good stick rotation and hand drive (both) out to the save.

Bounce Shots - Working the same arc, bounce overhand shots right at the keepers feet for 15-20 shots. Then bounce 15-20 shots (either side) 1-3 yards in front of the feet.

Anywhere - Do 15-20 shots to anywhere and be sure to be moving (driving, etc.) a lot by this point, but stay 10-14 yards out.

Big 5 - Challenge the goalie to 5 big outside shots to any-where and maybe buy him a soda if he gets 4 of 5.

Feeds
Add a feeder from behind and practice his stance facing the behind feeder and turning to the shooter on the pass. After doing 10 of these, move in to 4-5 yards out so that he can work on quick stick shot saves.

Add another player out front and pass the ball among the three players so that the keeper must work on his movement and footwork.

POOR TURNS (on feeds) are a common goalie weakness. Most of the warm-ups should be done with at least one feeder handling the ball on each shot, even if only one person (the coach) shoots. This helps the keeper be ready early after feeds so that he can get the STUFF saves sometimes needed in close games.

Drives
Pass from the side or behind and drive from 14 yards to 9/10 yards out shooting on the run.
End warm-ups with 3-5 drives from behind from each side to check his post position and saves.

More Reps
If the keeper wants some more reps on something, be sure that you give them. The coach can vary the difficulty to build confidence and

skill at the same time. If the keeper asks for something, it means that it is an area he feels needs work. If possible, the coach should help him then.

Caution

Warm-ups are instructive times in practice and are pre-game activities for games. Warm-up is not a shooting drill for anyone (especially offensive players). Wailing on the goalie by some salivating offensive players from 6 yards out is not warm-up, it is brutal. Caution your players to not do this. Organized shooting drills are needed, but they are not part of warm-up.

Encourage

During warm-ups re-enforce good stance (butt down, hands up, feet pigeon-toed), good positioning movement as well as saves. Encourage the keeper to pick it up in areas that he should be doing well (and already knows).

Talk

Have the keeper talk the shots as you warm him up. Talk to the keeper, help him get "up" for the game, it's as important, as technique. It is better for him, if he is flat, to get mad at the coach (he won't be flat) than for him to stay down. Pushing the keeper to a good intensity level is part of warm-up, especially on game day.

Teaching Time

During practice, some of the time is spent in working on a particular area of the keeper's game. Thus, in practice, warm-ups advice is given on how to improve where in game warm-ups the goal is to build confidence to play this game well (little or no teaching or new adjustments).

Backup

The team's other goalies should back-up the goal during their counterpart's warm-up. By watching the ball intensely, they can improve their concentration/reactions.

Changes

If the keeper has good pre-game warm-ups but is weak early in the game, change the warm-up. The warm-up may needs different shooters, more movement, some screens and more passing to better simulate game situations. This will also indicate that the goalie is not getting enough non-scrimmage repetitions and needs more pre-practice work using game-like drills.

Concentration

All keepers need to work on their continuity of concentra-tion. Some keepers are good on the save of the 1st shot in a sequence but are not ready for another shot or almost quit when the ball is on the ground leading to rebounds and second shot goals because of breaks in concentration.

The goalie can learn better concentration by teaching, as part of daily warm-ups, that the ball belongs to him until it is over the mid-line. If a ball come out of his stick, encourage him to run for it, scoop it up and throw a good, hard pass back to the warm-up shooter (or to an outlet player). If he takes his eyes off the shooter and the ball at any time shoot the ball into the goal (the harder the better) until the habit is broken and the keeper concentrates on goalkeeping for longer periods.

To re-enforce continuous concentration, use 6 shots and then have the keeper step out. Then do 6 more, in fairly rapid sequence including passes between a behind attackman and the out front shooter. This simulates game conditions better than shot after shot of warm-up.

Coach's Job   Before practice and during the team line drills or other similar time early in practice, one coach needs to work with the goalie, so that the keeper receives consistent instruction. Assistant coaches can handle the rest of the team. The head coach, usually the best coach, needs to work the keeper.

After Shot   During shooting warm-up, have the keeper pass the ball out to
Warm-up   another waiting player at the corner of the box (and then back to the shooter), so that the keeper works on his breakout passes during the shooting drill. After shooting warm-up, the keeper needs to practice long throws, especially on game days. This is usually done with the defense while the offense has shooting practice on the goal. On practice days, either the keeper joins the line drills or plays long catch with another goalie or coach.

C. Conditioning

Many people have kidded me about extending my playing career by moving from the coaches box to the goal as if there wasn't much difference. But, there is. The keeper has a demanding, tense job that saps energy as the game progresses. As the keeper becomes fatigued, reactions and attitude suffer. As Coach Vince Lombardi said;

"FATIGUE MAKES COWARDS OF US ALL."

So one big key to consistently good goaltending;

"GET IN SHAPE and STAY IN SHAPE !!!"

A keeper that is too tired to be effective in the last quarter has let his team down.

Strength   Goaltending is basically anaerobic (strength not endurance) oriented.

The primary key strength areas are the upper legs and the upper arms.

Developing the Legs

It is important to be on the balls of both feet the whole game supported mostly by the quadriceps muscles -- front large legs bent muscles on the top of the leg – and calf muscles – large muscles on the back of the lower leg.. Strength in these muscles carries the keeper through the game. There are tree ways to develop these muscles and anaerobic recovery;

1) weight training (leg presses and squats), <u>and</u>
2) wind sprints **up hill**.
3) jump over your stick handle 100 times per day

While weight training, it is important to also do hamstring curls so that there is balanced strength in the legs (otherwise a hamstring pull can occur).

The up hill wind sprints also develop the gluteus (butt), hamstring (rear upper leg) and calf muscles used to sprint to the end line after a missed shot. This sprint to the line can take a lot out of an already psyched-up goalie. Quick recovery from this sprint or a similar sprint during a clear is important to battling fatigue.

Developing Upper Arms

The second area to strengthen is the upper arms (deltoid muscles over the top of the shoulders). Once the stick begins to drop (below the level of 'looking-beside-the-thumb'), the keepers effectiveness drops.. These muscles are developed with weight training (military press and front lateral raise movements). As important is to run with the goalie stick and arms raised. This clearly uses the muscles in question. When running sprints uphill, run with the arms raised over the head and these muscles will develop also.

Stretching

Goalies need to stretch, possibly more than the running positions. They are subject to Achilles tendon injuries, back pain/injury and groin pulls more than most players. Warming the muscles up a bit before stretching (400-800 yard jog) will improve the impact of these stretches. The following stretches are used in sequence;

Butt stretch - sitting with the back against the wall and one leg braced with knee up, put the other ankle on the braced knee and pull this leg's knee to the nose (slowly for a 40 count). This pulls the gluteus (butt) muscles. Most back pain is due to the lower back muscles (spinal erectors) cramping because of tightness in the adjacent muscles (gluteus or upper back--trapezious and latissimus dorsi).

Upper back stretch - various stretches are used, the easiest is to grab a pole about two feet from the ground with one hand and from a squat push the butt away from the pole for a 40 count stetching the back's trapezious muscles.

Upper leg stretch - standing on one leg use the other side arm to grip the ankle and pull that leg to the butt for a 40 count. This stretches the quadriceps muscles of the upper leg (vastus medialis, vastus lateralis, et al). Do not flare the leg out (keep knee next to knee) or one can damage the hip.

Achilles / Upper Calf stretch - lean the whole body into a pole or fence with the foot flat on the ground and the knee locked. Rotate the hips forward and hold for a slow stretch 45-60 count. To accentuate the stretch place the free foot on the stretching foots Achilles tendon while stretching. This stretches the upper calf muscles (soleus and gastrocnemius).

Achilles / Lower Calf stretch - using the same stretch as above with a bent knee the Achilles tendons and the lower sections of the soleus muscles (lower calf) are stretched (use a 40 count). This stretch is vital to avoiding Achilles tendon injury and should be done after the calves have been stretched.

Groin stretch - sitting on the ground pull both feet to the groin while pushing the knees toward the ground. Hold for a 40 count. While in this position another player can push the back forward to increase the stretch.

Hamstring stretch - after all of these stretches then stand with feet farther than shoulder width apart and knees slightly bent bend the trunk over toward the ground and hang for a 40 count. (Do not lock the knee). This stretches the hamstring muscles (biceps femoris, et al).

If during this stretch you hold each elbow with the opposite hand that also stretches part of the upper back (trapezious) a second time. As the stretch finishes, lock the knee slowly for a 20 count. Do not let the muscles cramp (cramping is not stretching).

There are variations and other stretches that may work better for a specific individual, but using these will prepare most keepers for practice and games. Since all of these muscles are what are called "long" muscles, the stretch should be held for a long time 30-50 count to assure that "stretching" is really occurring.

Chapter 6
Shooters

Goalie's View

As a goalie, I first learned how to cover the goal and make saves. During the same years, I played some attack, mostly crease where I learned the shots and saves and scores of the game. As a keeper I realized that a keeper can make saves best when he is in position to make the save and can "see" the ball.

This chapter is written in part for shooters and in part for goalies. The goalies part includes three key lessons;

1) understand what the shooter is trying to do
2) visualize the shot/play when the ball is not in view
3) force the shooter into a "perfect" shot, the most difficult   shot under the circumstances.

Visualization

When the shooter hides the ball behind his back or helmet or behind a screen, the goalie needs to see through the player or screen to track the ball. This visualization is critical to consistent high level of play.

Shooter's View

The shooter's part of this chapter is meant to instruct coaches and players in what shots or shot formations are the hardest for the goalie to save. The difficulty for the goalie rises depending on how much of the goal he has to cover and/or how fast he has to react;

1) When the shooter has a low angle, or the shot is pretty far outside / in view, the goalie's job is easiest.
2) When the goalie has to move quickly into position or when the shooter is close/faking, the goalie's job is hardest because the shooter is "moving the keeper"
3) Bounce shots are harder to stop because the ball moves around on the bounce and the keeper must move the most body parts.
4) Overhand bounce shots are harder to stop than the underhand bounce shots because the shooter can do more overhand with the bounce than underhand where the keeper gets to see the ball longer.
5) Screen shots are hardest to stop since the ball is out of view for part of its flight
6) Shots made while the shooter is on the move are hard since the movement provides lot of distractions for the keeper to deal with.

Hiding the Ball   In traditional lacrosse, the game is played with passes that move at or just above the helmet. Today, we call that "playing at SIX FEET". With the ball at 6 feet above the ground it can be seen and easily distributed/shot in multiple directions (especially if the stick is vertical).

Since the 1990s, a large number of players have moved to playing the game with the stick head closer to the hip, are shooting underhanded or sidearm and are even flipping passes sidearm and underhanded to one another. Catching and shooting from the hip limits the shooters options -- an advantage to the goalie.

As the sticks have become better at ball control, the shooters have learned (from Paul Gait and Gary Gait and others) to counter the lack of options in some shots by hiding the ball behind their back or head.

This hiding not only interrupts the goalie's view of the ball, but disguises the shot. A side arm motion could yield an underhand (or even overhand) shot. This hiding the ball is effective, a sort of self-screen.

Keeper Counters   The keeper counters in three ways;

1) Visualize the ball through the player
2) Learn the shooters motion.
3) Wait to see the lip of the stick, the ball will appear earliest there, in time for an effective save.

By keeping concentration on the ball high, the stick motion can be followed until the ball re-appears. When it is not directly visible, visualize where it is and react accordingly. But, watching the ball/stick lip is more effective than learning the shooters motion.

A. Shots

Overhand Shots   The overhand shot is the hardest one for the goalie to defend because the shooter has so many options even late in his motion. By holding on to the ball longer, a bounce shot can result. An opposite corner shot is made by pushing out the bottom hand and twisting the head.

When an overhand shot (not side arm) is used, the ball can be passed to another player both easily and late. Once the goalie is committed to the overhand shooter, this player can almost freeze the keeper until late in his motion and either shoot or pass. Because of this, the goalie must watch-the-ball continuously (cuts down distractions). Once the shot has begun, goalies may guess and make a move to where the shot might go. Some keepers, on close-in shots might even CLOSE THEIR EYES, at this point. I had to learn to keep my eyes OPEN and focused ON THE BALL with both my top hand and eyes, then let my body follow to the ball. Trust the eyes/hand for good goal tending.

Overhand Bouncers

One form of overhand shot is very potent -- the overhand bounce shot. When the bounce shot is shot from helmet height (or above) with the stick vertical, the ball will skip to the left when it bounces (for a right handed shooter). Thus, the shooter can shoot wide of the pipe and have the ball move left into the net. This shot is unnerving because it looks wide and it is not. Some keepers may relax a little on this. By committing to saves on all shots, even those a bit wide, the keeper overcomes this.

Keeper's can also counter this through concentration, a strong step to the shot and a little move that covers the post with the hip. By practicing a slide of the hips toward the pipe, the goalie's upper body can cover the net near the pipe while the hands catch up to the shot.

Side Arm Shots

I used to think that the side arm shot was great as a goal tender. It seems easy to see and easy to save. But, the game has changed in the last years. Fast players that are cradling on the hip have developed an edge--the quick release side arm shot.

A case in point, was what Milford Marchant did to me. I was playing goal for the alumni in the Johns Hopkins Alumni Lacrosse game against the 1994 JHU varsity on Parents weekend in the fall 1993 at the end of "fall ball" for JHU. This was a thrill for me since I was one of four goalies for the alums and the other three super stars including Larry Quinn and Quint Kessinich.

Early in the first quarter, after an initial blocked shot and fast break by the alums, Milford Marchant cleared the ball back into our end, quickly set up right front cradling and looked at the right wing attackman (as did I). As I looked back at Milford, I saw the ball leave his stick coming under the arm of the defensive middie and eventually under my left arm into the goal. He had gotten off a high speed side arm shot right out of his cradle in the time it took me to look away and back again.

The goalie's defense against this shot is to pay attention by pointing the top hand at the ball. Now that you know it is a quick release shot, be prepared for it.

Underhand Shots Until 1994, I taught men goalies to play all but the very exceptional players low when the shooter dropped his hands for an underhand shot. Very few players had developed the strength and skill to accurately lift the ball up on an underhanded shot.

It is easier to lift the ball with the modern plastic sticks and pockets since the pocket is deeper and the ball feel is improved. It takes good form that consists of an under-hand shot where the shooters bottom hand finishes very near the elbow of the arm of the top hand (by lifting the bottom hand and pulling down and through to the top hand elbow). When you see this shot (instead of the shooter dragging both hands across the front of his body), then the side arm or underhand shooter has more control. More and more shooters have control high from a low hands position. Thus, this shot / save should be practiced as a regular part of warm-ups.

Learn the Shooters For keepers, the game is not just played one shot at a time. During the other team warm-ups, the keeper or the coach may study the other team's shooters to see if there is a good underhanded shooter and if so can he lift the ball to the upper corners. That shooter needs to be played with more focus and care than the other underhanded shooters. These other shooters will likely shoot low when they shoot sidearm or underhand.

Sidearm Bouncers The underhand or sidearm bounce shot is shot two ways. The first way the shooter keeps the stick head face roughly facing the goalie throughout. The second way, the shooter turns the stick face over as the ball comes out of the stick. This is sometimes called "turning your wrists over". Turning the wrists over imparts some topspin to the ball. In wet weather this topspin combined with the wet field will cause the ball to skip (stay low) when the shot bounces. If the keeper is not getting his stick all the way down to the ground during the save, then the ball may scoot under the keeper's stick (unexpect-edly) for a score. The goalie can learn this motion and compensate for the lower shot by sticking the stick head into the ground on low saves.

Close-in Shots in The closer the shooter is to the crease, the more he will do one of the following;

1) shoot high if the stick head is above the shoulder
2) shoot low if the stick head is below the hip
3) shoot for the short side (between the pipe and the goalie) when the angle is low

With this knowledge the coach/keeper work to cover part of the goal top with the stick when the hands are high, track the ball with the goalie's top hand throughout all the shooters motions and position to cut off the short side shot making the shooter make a "near-perfect" shot when in close and when defensive help is usually nearby.

Shot Results   The key to defending shots in close is to <u>watch-the-ball</u> and cover the places where he wants to shoot thus making the save or making the shooter change the shot. When the shooter changes the shot in close, he will;

1) miss some of the time
2) take more time allowing the defense to check the shooter in time to stop the score
3) take more time allowing the defense to check the shooter after the shot
4) drop the ball
5) sometimes score

Four of these are positive results. So, stay high when the shooter's hands are high covering the short side and go low when the stick is low covering the short side. Make the shooter make a move for the far pipe and the odds go up in favor of the goalie, even in close.

Front the Goal   Most of all, stay in the crease, in front of the goal, tracking the ball with the goalie's top hand and make the shooter shoot a very good shot. Running out to cream the shooter nearly always results in an easy dump by the shooter into an open net. At this point, the goalie can practice the "turn and rake" move used to retrieve the ball from the goal after the opponent has scored.

B. Screens

A screen is the positioning of one or more players between the shooter and the goalie for the purpose of interrupting the goalie's view of the shot. There are different kinds of screens, covered below.

Crease Screen involves the placement of a player (crease attack or middie) on the crease, in front of the keeper and occupying a defender (also in front of the keeper). The shooter looks to shoot around the screening player.

Crossing Screen involves having an offensive player cut between the shooter and the keeper just as the shot is released interrupting the goalie's view of the ball and making saving more difficult. This is a subtle screen that is nearly as disruptive as the Crease Screen.

Defender Screen Defender Screen involves shooting around the defender such that the defender's body hides the shot/ball from view. This is especially effective on a side arm bounce shot since this screen hides the ball effectively until it emerges from under the arm or off the hip of the defender limiting the goalie's reaction time.

Using Screens

Since the 1990's few teams screen well. This is particularly true at the high school level where few teams use a traditional (bulky, screening) crease attackman and few coaches teach middies and attack how to use the Crease or Crossing Screen. The 90's shooters, especially collegians, do use one screen effectively; the Defender Screen.

Offensive coaches with a couple of screen plays in the playbook provide an effective change-up. Screening and "moving" the goalie through planned cross-crease passes are offensive techniques that can overcome an otherwise strong goalie.

Looking Around Screens

Goal tending against screens is based on peeking around the screen and visualizing through the screen. By using the screen as part of what blocks the shooter's path to the goal, the goalie moves slightly out of position (toward one pipe or another) to see the shooter (looking around the screen). There is almost a boxer's bob and weave type of motion to peeking. Get a peek and then get back in position and then get another peek, etc. lowering the impact of the screen.

Moving the Screen

The other technique is to move the screening offensive player out from in front of the goalie. This is the defender's job in men's lacrosse (women have different rules here). When the goalie wants the screener moved, he asks the defender to, "Get him out of here" or "Move him Left (or Right)". Some pushing and shoving will commence where the defender pushes the offender into the crease, if possible, or to one side. A warning from the referee may result. But, unless the defender cross-checks the offender, it is unlikely that a penalty will be assessed. Using a little more than equal pressure will eventually tire out the screener and he will move away from the crease (or be pushed into it for a change of possession).

Defending Screens

The defense against the Crossing Screen and the Defender Screens is concentration where the goalie focuses such that when the ball is not in view it is nearly visible anyway. This "visualization" of where the ball is, is learned. For some, it is easily learned, for others it takes a lot of practice.

In warm-ups, especially for practice, use a Crease Screen (6 yards out) and a Defender Screen (8-10 yards out) close to the end of warm-ups. Also, the warm-up should have lots of shots where the ball is hidden (behind the body or the helmet) so that visualization (and searching for the stick lip for early ball seeing) can be done in warm-up. These activities provide practice and feedback time with the keeper almost every day.

C. Dodges and Motion

Tracking the ball (including tracking it using the top hand as a pointer) from an aggressive but balanced stance (knees bent, on the balls of the feet and leaning a bit forward in anticipation of going to the ball on the shot) is vital to effective goaltending.

There is a tendency in most keepers, especially when the shooter is closer to the goal, off of feeds or fakes for the keeper to pull the hands in and move his weight back onto his/her heels in a move that seems to be one of "blocking" the shot with the body. When this occurs, the shooter just has to shoot around the keeper, since the there is little "high speed" reaction ability left for the keeper (hands in or down and weight back). Goalies hands are faster when the top hand is at eye level and tracking the ball providing "high speed reaction" ability.

Watch the Ball   Most people when watching something don't watch it, they take a look and look away, then take another look or glimpse at the ball. Real goaltending is more like a stare-down contest between two people only one of them is the ball. Anything that interrupts that level of concentration, deep enough to see the ball spin, is a distraction.

Distractions   A save can be made in about ¼ second and a shot can be released in about ¼ second but, if goalie eye/hand contact with the ball is lost then that takes about ¼ second to regain giving a big advantage to the shooter. With this in mind, distractions that loose eye/hand contact with the ball are destructive to effective goaltending.

The biggest form of distraction is motion; usually in the form of a fake, a running shot or major change of stick position (switching hands, high to low to high, etc.). The most difficult change of stick position is a split dodge since in a split dodge the shooter changes hands and direction interrupting any body language that the keeper might use to determine the shot and many times leading to a defensive pull-back by the keeper (hands in or weight back or both).

Counteracting Distractions   Practicing countering distractions is based upon working on the major distractions and staying aggressive to the ball and staying in contact with the ball (watching the ball with the top hand as a pointer). The best ways to build this ability to be "in-the-shot" on

every shot, even those very close to the crease, is to successfully
practice saves that incorporate those characteristics by using the

1) Six Yard Drill (see drills)
2) Six Yard Drill with motion where the ball is moved from one side
   to the other (either changing hands or not) so that ball tracking is
   critical to being able to react to the shot.
3) Six Yard Drill with split dodges similar to the above
4) Drive Drills from up top shooting at 8-9 yards out.
5) Drive Drills from up top with split dodges shooting at 8-9 yards
   out
6) Drive Drills from behind shooting at 5 yards above GLE and 5
   yards outside the post on either side
7) Drive Drills from behind with fakes and roll dodges to work on
   concentrating on the ball, not the motion.
8) Drive Drills from GLE with split dodges to work on the motion
   and position needed.

The outcome expected is to build a progression of successes by
getting a single save and then one save out of five and then two or
three out of five – for each type of motion/dodge save. This builds
the confidence that the keeper can be more than just a blocker
on close in shots and is the foundation for being an impact player
against teams that can get the ball close to the goal.

CHAPTER 7
ATTITUDE AND CONCENTRATION

Goaltender is a critical position to a lacrosse team. The objective of the goalie and defense is to get the ball and get it back to the offense; starting a fast break if possible.

The goalie is involved in 30-60 chances a game where the opposition could score. That is more chances per game than any other position on the field. The team needs production from the position. It is a different position than attack, middie or even defense because it is the last line of defense. As Bob Scott said, "it is a vital position." Coaches need to teach it in a way that produces a pivotal ball player, if possible.

A. Attitude

Mental Position   The goalie position is more of a MENTAL challenge than a physical challenge. For many players and keepers the position is scary from two points of view; fear of failure and fear of being hurt. Both are real emotions. It is mandatory that they not only be managed but overcome, since **impact** goaltenders:

- **attack** the shot, make the **save**
- help **direct** the defense
- get **ground balls**
- **pick off** some feeds
- **aggressive**ly play the ball/pass
- actively **clear** the ball
- **run out** shots that are wide or high
- **start** the fast break
- **inspire** their teammates by their winning and combative attitudes.
- occasionally make **big saves**

Take Charge Keepers   We need leadership in between the pipes. Who hasn't had keepers who weren't "in the game" and the defensive tone went flat. A coach or team can survive this cagainst weak teams, but against strong teams, they will attack harder. Good defenses attack the offense starting in goal.

Since the keeper can't stop everything, defense needs to keep the offense out of particular positions. When the defense keeps the offense out of the dangerous zones in front of the goal, the keeper needs to believe that the shooter CAN'T score. When the offense gets into the dangerous zones, the keeper needs to see this as an opportunity to make one of those STUFF saves that the team occasionally needs to win big games.

Next Shot

No matter what the outcome, a save, a miss, a score, the keeper has to have the attitude that the NEXT shot is going to be his save. **He or she must put aside whatever has happened and move onto the next play.** It is critical to make that move to the next play NOW, no lapses. That's part of a winning attitude. When a team gives up goals in bunches either they get DOWN or SLOPPY as a team or the goalie gets DOWN or SLOPPY. The keeper needs to manage his attitude, move to the next save, reset his intensity and focus at lifting the team back up.

Whining is not Winning

anywhere, and it is nearly fatal inside the crease.

Keeping Up -Self Talk

There are tricks, tips, techniques, clichés and methods for keeping your attitude up. But, the best way is to talk positively to oneself. A most important fact in life is;

You Get What You Say To Yourself

Talking to yourself, out loud, is a great way to reset yourself and your expectations so phrases like;

Get the Next One   **Watch The Ball**
Hands Up   **Butt Down**
Wrists to the Back   **Point toes (at the shooter)**
Set up early

all work to refocus and be ready on the next shot.

Another good technique is to partner with someone. The best keepers have a partnership with a couple of team-mates and the goalie coach where they encourage one another. Partners build and rebuild a winning attitude with our keepers even during a game.

Jeff & Jon II

This is not just a matter for young people. In 1994 at the Vail Masters Tournament, in the incredible MVP game that I mentioned earlier,

Jeff Singer, my friend and teacher was on the sidelines. It was not silent support. He is a quiet man, but every few minutes I could hear his encouragement. Some of it was recognition of a good play and some was a tip or two for me to use to adjust better to the game at hand. I am thankful for both the friendship and the comments, they carried me through that (and other) games.

B. Concentration/Focus

Managing Lapses Concentration is built in many ways and comes in various forms. Goalies and coaches know when concentration is lacking. If lapses in concentration coincide with shots by the opposition, the result is a goal. It is not great shots or great passes by the offense that beats goalies. Goalies know when the other team earned their score. Other scores are because the goalie was distracted.

Results of Lapses Goalies know when they let a goal in or maybe could have made the save. Most goalies know that they were not focused at the task at hand resulting in;

1) **Not being ready to play**
2) **Taking one's eye off the ball**
3) **Not taking a step (to attack the shot)**
4) **Being out of position**

Thus, the keys to good concentration are ways to watch the ball, be ready to play, and take a step toward the shot. I use key words" **Watch, Ready, Go, Next**" to reinforce the things about making saves that the goalie can control and the words that they can say to themselves to improve concentration and performance.

Focus Tips Many of the techniques and tips for retaining or regaining concentration are useful. I bang my stick on my face mask, reset my stance and raise my hands and then I look for the seam in the ball. Yes, I look for the seam in the ball. Almost every lacrosse ball has a seam that is a residual from the ball manufacturing process. The key for the coach and the keeper to understand is this;

WHEN YOU CAN SEE THE SEAM IN THE BALL, YOU ARE TRULY CONCENTRATING

Big Games In 1993, I was warming up before the Lacrosse Classic North / South Old Timer's All-Star game at Johns Hopkins, fully expecting to see my old friend, Geoff Berlin (JHU '68) show up and start the game for the South in goal. As the warm-up progressed through my normal sequence, I noticed that I was SEEING everything. I could see the ball in the stick and I could see it bounce and I could see it spin and I could see the seam in the ball. Geoff's business kept him away and I got my first start on Homewood field.

That day, I saw the ball as well as I ever had and made save after save after save that resulted in our winning the game (16-8) and my being awarded the MVP. Brooks Sweet (All World 1984 attackman who played for the North team) and I laughed and laughed together because he had to work for every score and quite a few shots were rejected because I could SEE.

This level of concentration is <u>acquired</u>, that means that you can teach it and the keeper can learn it. There are a number of techniques, as follows;

Playing for 30 Seconds

Most goals involve the goalie being distracted, by a fake, by a screen, or by inattention to the ball.

When a goalie is stabbing at the ball during the shot and/or dropping his head after the play, take time to talk to him about continually watching the ball (even when it is at the other end of the field) and playing for 30 seconds at a time (not just 2-3 seconds at a time). During warm-ups, work up to 30 second sequences (5 or 6 shots) before taking a break. This reinforces the importance of concentration and avoids some of the distraction that result in goals. An important consequence is that it raises the keeper's intensity, keeps him/her in a solid ready stance (helping avoid lapses) and therefore raises the level of play.

Goalies with good quickness take breaks at strange times. One goalie that I coached had hands so fast that once he realized that he was going to make the save he would take a break while the ball was **in flight**. This break in concentration cost goals. We sat down and I talked with him about his excellent physical skills and his poor concentration. We changed his approach from one of being excited because he thought he was going to save the ball to one where he would watch the ball all the way until it hit his goalie stick pocket. He wasn't going to be a good goalie until he could raise his concentration above his physical skills. As he began to understand that I saw good potential in him, he worked and got better.

Watch-The-Ball

The first technique is to "watch the ball". This means watch the ball -- not watch the player, the fake, the pick, the stick, the eyes, the helmet, the motion, the move, the defender or the hit. It means literally to **watch-the-ball**.

Stance

Part of concentration is having the best stance for the shot taken, when it is taken – being ready to go to the shot. By constantly adjusting the stance (feet, knees, back, arms, hands and stick) the keeper's brain is computing the best stance for the situation, second to second. This using your brain to re-evaluate, adjust and re-adjust adds to concentration.

Standing flat-footed, waiting for the play to come nearer and then setting up, usually results in setting up late. Setting up late denies the keeper the comfort of the adjust and re-adjust activities and thus makes the keeper a little edgy (positively edgy to go) as the shot flies.

Setting Up Early What many keeper's don't understand (but can learn) is that all the good things that can be done before the shot CAN MAKE THE SAVE EASIER (or possible). Once the shot begins, there is no time left to get good balance or move to a better position. Therefore, prepare for every shot, so that the least movement is needed to make the save. The less movement required the higher chance of making the save ("Smooth is Fast").

If the shooter hits you and you didn't move then your set-up was perfect. Even though the keeper wants to make the save with the stick and wants to step to every shot, from a stance and position point of view, getting hit is better than getting scored upon.

Hands The part that is critical about the hands is that the more they start high the more fluid the body is to the ball. Hands are fastest when the top hand is on a line between the eye and the ball (but not blocking the top hand eye's vision of the ball). SMOOTHNESS to the ball is what we are striving for (along with range) to improve the keeper's game. Letting the keeper cheat by keeping his hands low or close to the chest really hurts hand speed, ability to concentrate and fosters "stabbing" at the ball (another bad habit). Working with the keeper to "look-beside-the-thumb" not only helps speed, concentration and smoothness but gives the coach a simple piece of advice when the keeper needs to reset his concentration during a game (HANDS UP or THUMB or EYE-THUMB-BALL).

Bang / Clang Whenever I get to over-thinking in goal (including thinking about my stats, food after the game, what happened on the last shot, my position, etc.) and there is a break in play, I will BANG my stick on my face mask, then on the pipe on either side and then on my face mask, hard, four or five times and talk out loud to myself. This gets the cobwebs out and helps me focus.

After playing goal for a while I learned that saves where the ball hits the helmet cage don't hurt and are exhilarating. That great CLANG and then a cheer from the stands seems to say something about

HANGING IN THERE as a goalie. So CLANGING the face mask gets me going again too. It is not good technique but produces an acceptable result – no goal.

The first time that you tell your goalie to grasp the stick with his hands about 18 inches apart and to bash his face mask with the part of the shaft between his hands, he is likely to look at you like you are crazy. Something like, "I'm not doing that in front of my friends" may go through his mind. You can say something like, "I know it sounds crazy but your friends already think you're crazy for playing goal so what's a little craziness between friends." or "Coach Weston says it works so try it." or you could explain about the CLANGING on a face mask save. This technique is not for everyone, but it works great for me and a few other keepers, so maybe it will work for you.

Position

Constant re-evaluation, adjustment and re-adjustment of the stance adds to concentration. This is also very true for position. Position is the placement of the goalkeeper's body, limbs, head and stick in the crease so that the shooter has as little goal to shoot as possible.

A common lapse in concentration that a keeper makes is being in the wrong position. The most common wrong position is to leave an opening between the pipe and the keeper's body for the shooter to score on the short side.

Playing the Pipe

The most effective adjustment in position that the keeper can make is to choose which side is the short side and adjust to that side. The less angle the shooter has the more the pipe needs to be covered. Part of position is to assure that while the pipe is played that it does not become a hindrance to a good move to the ball or cause a stance that locks one knee.

The keeper's rear-end is not IN the goal when one plays close to the pipe, the body is a half step out from the pipe so that full motion is available to move to the ball on the shot. If the helmet is used on the pipe side for the save, then lean the head there late in the shot (don't lean on the pipe before the shot, it messes up the stance and smoothness to the ball).

The keeper can also test his position in relation to the pipe by tapping the pipe with the stick. This is helpful and is superior to looking at the pipe (and therefore away from the ball) to determine the position. But, banging the stick on the pipe during play drops the hands away from good position leaving the goalie vulnerable to a quick shot before his hands are returned to just below the chin.

Using Markers

Most marking of the crease does not work for maintaining position inside the crease. Yes, kicking out spots in the crease line at 12 o'clock, 10 o'clock and 2 o'clock doesn't work since the keeper has to look down from the field of play to pick up these markers.

But, the off field marker or reference point really works, in a different way. As the keeper takes his position at the beginning of the period, he should pick out three reference points in the distance (viewable without looking down) at 12 o'clock (usually the other goal) for centering ones self during fast breaks and other times, at 2-3 o'clock to reference the right pipe and at 9-10 o'clock to reference the left pipe. At one end of the field these reference points can be determined and even practiced during warm-ups. Their advantage is that the keeper can see them without looking down or looking at the pipe (both breaks in focus on the ball). Thus, markers (in the distance) help one avoid other distractions while working on correct positioning in the goal.

Bounce, even Scream

Chet Speed played goalie at Landon School (Potomac, MD), Colgate University and for many years as a star in for the Washington Lacrosse Club. Chet is one of those friends and personalities that one never forgets. To say that Chet is hyper during a game is an understatement. He gets all wound up and plays with tremendous intensity that fires him up and fires up the rest of the team. Every player that played with Chet knows that Chet is completely focused and concentrating on the game, the defense and mostly on goaltending (not the women on the sidelines?).

During the play, Chet bounces in the goal. He bobs and weaves, jumps and bounces, constantly adjusting his position and maintaining his focus on the ball and the play. Chet's key to success is that he is IN every shot; he is ready, positioned and focused for every shot, every dodge, every slide, every screen and every pass. You would like to have him on your team too.

Relax Breaks

Another concentration technique is to "concentrate" then "relax". The goal position cannot be played for a whole game concentrating continuously. There are times to be ready and there are times to relax. Most goals are shots that were missed by the goalie because he was distracted at the critical moment.

MOST GOALS ARE SHOTS THAT WENT IN
BECAUSE THE GOALIE WAS NOT READY

Some of these times are after initial excellent saves where the keeper does not reset for the rebound shot. Some of these distractions involve screens. Some involve thinking about the last save/goal. Some involve relaxing during the shot since it is obvious that you can make the save. I have heard this called "going to sleep during the shot." It happened to me in a Lake Placid tournament in a close game. It was a low, slow shot that I could easily save, but I moved too slow to be in front of the shot and it bounced in, just because I took a break during the shot.

The key is relaxing (taking a deep breath and gathering oneself for the next play) when the play is stopped or up-field or for a "not dangerous" ground ball in the far corner behind. By concentrating for 30 seconds at a time, the keeper's overall concentration will remain high. Then one of these "relax" or "break" opportunity will arise. During the 30 seconds, the keeper pushes all his concentration buttons (stance, watching the ball, hands up, knees bent, bounce, TALK, TALK, TALK, etc.) to stay on top of the play and the ball until a save, pick-off, ball out of bounds or "break" happens.

C. Talking

Talk, Talk, Talk   Some goalies learn a great secret and some never do. That secret is:

**"The team and the goalie play better
if the goalie <u>talks</u> to the defense"**

Under Goal Play, I cover what kinds of talk help the individual defenders and what team talk helps the overall defense. The secret is one of communication for <u>teamwork</u> **and** talking for <u>concentration</u>.

Ah! Petramala   For example, I had the opportunity to play goal in back of a great defense that included Dennis Townsend (JHU) and Dave Petramala (JHU) against the JHU 1994 Varsity. As the play developed, Terry Riordan (JHU's all-time leading scorer) was being defended by Dave behind the goal. I called to Dave "Left Behind" and "Left Behind". As Terry came to the pipe, "Left Pipe" and as he moved up field "Left Side, Left Side" and then asked Dave for help by saying "Hold". ("Hold" means that the shooter is in a seriously dangerous shooting position and should not be allowed to move toward the goal any further.) **DAVE STRIPPED THE BALL** from Terry. I was awed by his ability and our teamwork. Later, Dennis did the same thing to the other wing against attackman Dave Marr under almost the exact circumstances.

Avoiding Saves by Talking

Each time the defenseman and the goalie were in synch. The keeper helped the defenseman regarding the ball position and the dangerousness of the shooter's position. The defender responded by choosing his move at just the right moment. After some years of playing goal, I realized that the save I don't need to make, (because the defense blocks the shot, steals the ball, or gets a ground ball) is the best defensive play of all. Thus, my attitude and my concentration is heightened when I talk to and help the defense with position and slide calls.

An important technique is to use the first name of the defender in your calls, "Hold him, JIM". This increases the defender's concentration. It also develops the closeness needed in a good defensive unit.

A quiet goalie loses the talk advantages and needs to be taught how to talk with the defense without interfering with the goalie's concentration. This takes practice. It is so important that I suggest that the goalie talk about check, rebound, clear, ball position, the pass, etc. during goalie warm-up and throughout practice so that everyone is used to it as a part of the team defensive scheme.

There is a balance here. Talk is a vital part of goalie play. Too much talk will be ignored or nearly ignored by the defense. By giving the defense concise and useful information, they will respond. Over-talking can cause them to tune out and treat the keeper's calls as background noise.

D. Seeing

More than Looking

What does this "SEEING" mean? It is a form of concentration that produces tunnel vision and slows the game down for the keeper. The keeper sees the ball sooner and clearer and moves smoother and quicker to each shot. SEEING is much more than just looking; it is focusing on the ball so that the keeper can:

1) See it rotate; even see the seam on the ball.
2) Visualize the ball even when the shooter hides the ball behind his body or helmet.
3) Visualize the ball even through a screen so that the screen does not distract the keeper from being in the correct position or knowing when the ball is shot.
4) Avoid being distracted by head fakes, shoulder fakes, eye fakes or pass/shot fakes by pointing at the ball in the stick with the top hand.
5) Move smoothly to the ball.

6) Feel that the ball and the overall play is "slowed down" to the point that it is in "slow motion".

Slow Motion
When the keeper gets so focused on the ball that this "slow motion" feeling sets in, then the keeper is SEEING and also seems to have plenty of time to get to the shot or get to the pass or make the save. Coaches and keepers need to search for and strive for that level of play. It begins with and ends with an intense concentration on the ball.

Tracking the Ball
There are tricks to maintaining focus and concentration. Watch the ball ALL THE TIME; in the air, in the players pocket, off the lip of the stick, in flight toward the goal and into the goalie stick pocket. From the initial warm-up until the last whistle, know exactly where the ball is.

Jeff Singer watches by watching the HEAD of the STICK. He says that if he can see the ball at the point that it leaves the shooter's stick then he has a high probability of stopping the shot.

Almost Missed Shutout
Playing in a summer league game, our whole team, the Virginia Gray Beards, was playing well. In the third quarter, we had a shutout going against the Navy Goats. Shutouts are very rare between good teams so we were working hard to keep that DONUT (shutout). I was in a "zone" seeing everything and enjoying the game, even though Bobby Chancellor had had one of his two saves as a defenseman already. As the third quarter ended, a Navy defenseman threw a full field shot at the goal. I lost it in the lights and it went between my legs into the goal.

But, the clock had run out--no goal. We held them and got the shutout that day. Each time in goal that I think about taking a break or not watching the ball, I remember that game and concentrate on the ball again. In 42 years, I have seen only four shutouts and played in only two. For our team that day all but 5 guys had never played in one either. I will never forget it or how close I came to messing it up.

Keep Watching
Keep watching the ball itself, not the player, or the play or the defense, **Watch-the-Ball**. It makes a difference

CHAPTER 8
COACHING GOALIES

Positive Attitude One of those "positive attitude" writers has a catchy phrase that seems to apply to coaching goalies.

> **"People need to know that you care before they care what you know. "**

Goaltender can be a lonely and a critical position. Befriending your goalie(s) may be your best way of coaching them. You don't need to have them over for dinner, but if they know that they are not all alone between the pipes, that they have your support, then they will improve. Caring is important.

A. Making Changes

Progress & Performance There is a delicate balance that a coach maintains as he/she works with keepers. This balance is between progress and performance. Changing a goalie's approach, technique or style is a progressive thing. It is a little like building a wall out of bricks -- laying a couple of bricks every day is better than doing a wall in one day.

When you suggest a change in grip or position, for a while after that the goalie may not play as well. As he assimilates the instruction performance will improve.

This is not always so that performance will temporarily degrade, especially when the instruction smoothes out an area that is already a positive part of the tender's play. But, where a larger <u>change</u> in play is required, (i.e. change in stance or steps), it is very important to consider when to make the adjustment. For example, no significant instruction or change should be introduced during a pre-game warm-up.

It is best to introduce changes in summer lacrosse camp, during fall ball or in the first few days of spring practice. There are times when you have to make mid-season changes, generally because the goalie's performance is declining or is below par. When you do, make sure that there are 3-4 practices to work out the changes and lots of practice time with the keeper so that he can get as comfortable as possible with the changes prior to having to perform in a game.

Building for Adjustment

This is not to say that adjustment isn't necessary, even in games. Goalies, maybe more than any other player, tend to "go south", "tune out", "have a bad day", or "go sour" for parts or all of games. It is important that coaches catch them as they slide down in performance. Teaching something in practice as a foundation gives the coach a chance to help them "get back in the game".

For most goalies, lapses in concentration can be overcome by five simple rules;

Adjustment Rule 1 - Teach the keeper something basic that is re-enforced in almost every practice that can be re-emphasized during warm-ups and games. I usually focus at parts of the stance (raising the hands or pointing the toes inward), concentrating on (or "seeing") the ball, or playing the pipe.

Adjustment Rule 2 - Talk to the goalie regularly during practice and games to re-enforce good saves, recovering from the last shot to be ready for the next, good outlet passes, etc. This builds a positive communication between you.

Adjustment Rule 3 - Yell / go nuts (cheer your keeper heartily) on a good to excellent save. He will glow from your appreciation of his contribution (as will the team).

Adjustment Rule 4 - When you need to, tell the keeper something, tell him only <u>ONE</u> basic point to get ready for the next shot. Goalies spend a lot of time thinking when the play is on the other end and can tend to "out-think" themselves. Giving too much game time instruction is also a distraction. Giving him ONE thing he can FOCUS on may get him back in the game.

For example, good advice is "Watch the BALL". If this needs embellishment, then I might add, "You are watching the shooter, watch the BALL!!."

Another area is directing the defense where one might instruct, "Talk to the Defense, let's hear you !!"

Adjustment Rule 5 - Get ready for the next shot. It is vital to work with the goalie to keep him from "getting down" on un-savable shots or even shots he should have saved. Indicate that the next shot is the important one and help him recover to lead the team on the next series.

Become the keepers best cheerleader at the same time as coaching and the keeper will continued to improve.

B. Evaluating Performance

Save %-age   The most obvious way of evaluating a keeper's performance is either wins/losses or save percentage. I do believe that the better goalies have the better save percentages. This is calculated by:

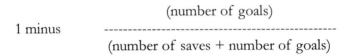

$$1 \text{ minus } \frac{(\text{number of goals})}{(\text{number of saves} + \text{number of goals})}$$

Generally, in high school, a good save percentage is one above 67% and a bad one is below 55%. College save percentages below 60% is bad and above 70% is exceptional.

There are a lot of team factors that go into save percentage. Therefore, it may not be the best way to evaluate goaltender performance. Here is an effective evaluation / rating system to judge a good game play:

STUFFS - Count the number of **STUFFS** (impossible saves) that the keeper had in the game. All one-on-one saves are stuffs and most saves where the opposition is screening the goalie qualify. A save on a shot eight yards or closer should be counted.

The goalie has the advantage on the shooter when the shot originates from 13-14 yards out or farther. The shooter has the advantage from 12 yards in or closer. So an 8 yard save is definitely a STUFF since a STUFF is a save that the keeper isn't supposed to be able to make.

FAST BREAK Starts - Count the number of **FAST BREAKS** that are started by the keeper. Generally, the keeper has to get the ball to start breaks and generally, this means he has made the save. But, if the ball does not make it to the mid-line then the save may have been in vain. Since the keeper has it within his power to do more than just toss the ball to the defense, starting the break is the best outcome once he has gotten the ball.

GROUND BALL, PICK-OFF, SHOT RUN-OUT - Count 1/2 point each when the goalie that gets the ball back for your team

MISSES - Count the number of times that the keeper missed a save that should have been made

THROWAWAYS - Count the number of times that the keeper threw the ball away (bad pass or dropped catch) that the keeper should have made

TURNOVERS – Count the number of times the keeper turns the ball over outside the goal (beyond throwaways)

Calculate Performance

The higher the number that is the result of the better game the keeper had.

STUFFS plus FAST BREAK STARTS plus 1/2 of GROUND BALLS, PICKOFFS and RUNOUTS minus MISSES and THROWAWAYS and ½ of GOALIE TURNOVERS

Positive is Positive

A **+10** is excellent unless there are 3 or more MISSES or THROWAWAYS. This is an IMPACT PLAYER performance A **+5** is good to very good. A minus game is a poor performance.

There are very few shutouts in lacrosse. Sometimes the offense earns their goals. Sometimes a keeper shines in a loosing cause and sometimes may play poorly in a winning cause. Even in a blowout, this little equation helps the keeper objectively understand his contribution regardless of the outcome.

One caution--don't get too zealous in counting. Precision is not key here. Clear understanding of overall performance is. Any count that is positive is a good day and any keeper who has a good attitude at the end of a tough day is worth working with some more.

C. Teaching Structure

I believe that many coaches teach their sport through bulk repetitions. For team practices of middies, attack and defense, there is a lot to this approach. For goalies, the game is not so much learning physical moves. It is a MENTAL game for goalies; one of angles, confidence, concentration, visualization, focus and attack. Everything that a goalie is taught needs a context that builds, not destroys, confidence in how he tends goal.

Embracing Instruction

What is most important to teaching a goalie is that he accept the instruction, try the change and then embrace it as an improvement. We can get this level of acceptance by two techniques; explanation and affirmation. The explanation is the hardest part because we as coaches may have seen good technique but don't know how to explain why one technique is superior. If that happens to you call a good goalie and talk it over. That input will help you explain it to him and add to your credibility.

Explanation

For example, most goalies will set up in their stance with their feet splayed slightly outwards (a little slew footed). Good technique involves them setting up a little pigeon toed. With the feet a little splayed, the foot needs to be turned (toward pigeon toed) before the keeper can drive off that foot. If it is already pointed inward, then the keeper can drive without lifting the foot and turning it first. This saves a lot of reaction time (Tip from Guy Van Arsdale). Once explained, most keepers adjust to this stance immediately.

In a similar way, work with the keeper's throwing. The keeper's feet during a save are not in position to throw the ball after the save. By changing the whole stance after the save to a throwing stance, more accuracy, distance, power and throw control is gained. Showing the keeper how to throw in this different stance and explaining the increased capability and the importance of good throwing to starting the fast break helps the keeper embrace this jump into a throwing stance after the save.

Affirmation

Once we have introduced something to the keeper, we need to re-enforce it. When you see it, tell the keeper that you see it. For example, tell him that the new stance is "working" or "going to pay off". Say something to acknowledge his effort to use the technique.

Verbalization

One key affirmation that provides a basis for communications are questions;

"Do you understand that ?"
"Does that make sense to you ?"
"Do you think that you can use this ?"
"Are you comfortable with this ?"
"I can see the difference. Can you feel the difference?"

If they don't understand, if it doesn't make sense, if there is no perceived difference, eventually the keeper will tell you and then you can work on the area of misunder-standing, accommodation or adjustment. By having the keeper speak to you, he verbalizes and gains confidence.

Learn Yourself

Goal keeping is constant adjustment by the keeper. He adjusts to the shooter, to the shot, to where the ball is on the field, etc. But, there is a deeper adjustment within.

A good goal keeper learns about himself to the point that he can
see what he is doing wrong (physically or mentally) and correct
or adjust the attitude, concentration, stance, hands, position, etc.
so that whatever was wrong is corrected BEFORE THE NEXT
SHOT. Coaches can tune some of this, but the best coaching is one
that teaches the keeper to recognize what is going on and correct it
himself. Having the keeper verbalize what you are pointing out helps
the keeper's learning and the adjustments that he can make.

Not for Everybody For some keepers, the changes in technique or style that you are
trying to make will not work for them. As a coach, you need to
decide whether to restart the instruction or to adjust in some other
area with the keeper. Not all good tips are for all keepers. It may be
better to work on some other area than to alienate the keeper by
continually emphasizing something that does not yet fit into his style.
Good coaches have to deal with this reality as positively as possible.

**Sandwich
Discussions** If, as I have supposed, goal keeping is a mental game centered on
confidence, how we introduce changes to a keeper is critical. I try
to make everything positive (although I am not very tolerant of less
than a full effort). Thus, everything is couched as an improvement.
Most of the improvements are to range (the ability to effectively
cover more of the goal area), smoothness and angles that lower
the possibility of the shooter scoring. Thus, put the instruction
in a sandwich -- something good, some instruction, followed by
something good.
For example,

"Your reaction was good, but you stepped backward, so let's step forward to improve"

Here, the "stepped backward" bad part is in between two positives.
It's like a sandwich where the good is the bread and the bad or
instruction is the jelly. This makes communication easier and makes it
more reasonable and easier for the keeper to embrace the instruction
than;

"Step forward, can't you ever step into the shot!"

This is a confidence bruiser and bad coaching, where sandwich dialog
is easier for the athlete to manage.

**Too Soft or
Too Hard** For those of you who have a strong authoritative style that is
definitive and pointed, you may feel somewhat put off by this
"Too Soft" discussion. But, I would have you review how you have
felt when someone has recognized how well you coached even
when your team lost. The fact that your team lost is not gone, but

the recognition that you did well with the team is still much more welcome than criticism or second guessing.

Most coaches that work with me at clinics so that they can manage their goaltenders better are already good coaches. So I couch everything in terms of improvement (NOT RIGHT or WRONG) so that the coach can <u>embrace</u> the techniques and tips.

If I said, " Just have the kid do this . . or that . ., **cause I said so**. ", then most coaches would ignore the instruction (if not tell me to "buzz off" or worse).

Goalies are independent specialists on our teams. It is important to treat them just like we want to be treated when we go to clinics, etc. A little softer delivery coupled with a consistent and persistent message works better if we want to have the athlete hold up when the going gets tough in crucial games.

D. Tips From the Cage

Positive over Negative

The goalkeeping position is inherently negative. As coaches, your keeper needs to hear a lot of positive to help overcome it. Your faith in him, persistence and patience is the basis for the development of your keeper. Positive inputs, even about a poor game, really helps.

Coach or Wait

There are times to coach and times to wait. Many keepers do not want to hear much coaching from the sidelines during games. For many, it's embarrassing. If comments aren't encouraging then they may have to wait. As valuable as time-outs are in a game, I have used more than one to talk with the keeper out of earshot of fans and other players.

Some of this involves a coach's style. Even in practice, I will walk across the field to the player in order to make my comments about something that he is doing wrong. I like encouragement and complements to be loud and public and criticism and changes to be more private.

With keeper's, this situation is amplified. Many have flashes of depression when they miss a makable save or botch a pass and the other team scores. Theirs is a very public position with, in their minds, some public embarrassment involved when they miss. Coaches need to think twice about further embarrassment when considering when and how to advise their keepers.

Get Help, It Helps If your keeper is not progressing, get some help for him. Not all relationships between keepers and coaches are effective. Someone else's eyes may see something that can be corrected (mechanics, position, attitude, concent-ration) and someone else's voice can communicate it to the goalie. Keepers and keeper coaches are a close lot, so if you ask one of us, it is likely that we will find the time to work with your keeper. If you do, I will.

CHAPTER 9

ADVANCED TOPICS

Lots of Basics   Goaltending can be very basic and much of what is in this book is basic. But, there is a lot to know to be good at every facet of the position. That is why the book feels a bit long when one considers that it only covers one position--goalie. There are some advanced topics. This chapter is meant to provide some of the instruction that is advanced at the high school level but is more normal at the higher levels of college and post-college club play.

A. Managing the Defense

Defense is a major part of the game of lacrosse. There are many excellent defensive sets, maneuvers and techniques. This area of the book is not meant to teach the finer points of lacrosse defense but to look at it from a goaltender's point of view. There are really three parts to this point of view:

Appreciation -- Every save that wasn't made because the defense prevented the shot, got a ground ball, made a clear, etc. should be appreciated. Very rarely does a keeper win a ball game on his own. The fewer chances to make a save the offense has the better the chances that the team is going to win.

Understanding -- There are defensive moves/plays, just like goalie moves, that don't work. Even though these mis-plays are frustrating, keepers need to understand that sometimes these plays happen and the keeper needs to get past them to the next save or play.

Adjustment -- There are sets, positioning, slides, clears that don't work well, but can work with adjustment. Not all adjustment comes from the coaches, partly because they do not see what the keeper sees.

The keeper can adjust the defense, especially, if he is allowed to by the coaches, knows the adjustments available and if he can build the rapport with the defense players needed to have the adjustments work. The advanced keeper can be a real asset in this area and the best coaches will encourage the keeper along lines consistent with the coaches defensive approach.

The defense protects the hole, giving up only the outside shot

What to Change There are group of individual defensive actions that can result in no save being needed:

- Picking off a pass
- Knocking down the offensive player
- Taking the ball away from the offender
- Blocking a shot
- Causing a ground ball
- Picking up a ground ball
- Making a clear

These individual moves should be cheered by the keeper, when successful. But, attempting some of these can jeopardize the team defense. A missed take-away check many times results in a close-in shot by the offense. So, the keeper and the coaches need to work with the defenders to be patient regarding some of these so that the team defense can be effective.

Best, Better, Good The keeper and the coaches need to be able to communicate with the defense as to what is desired generally and what specifically is needed for this game or against this type of personnel. For example,

- The keeper is most vulnerable when the shooter is within 8 yards, is centered in front of the goal, has no one guarding him and/or the goalie is screened.
- The keeper is least vulnerable, except for those times when the ball is at the other end of the field, when the shooter is farther out than 12 yards, is on the side of the goal and the defender is applying pressure to the bottom hand or has the offensive stick head covered.

Knowing this allows the coaches to generate a set of danger zones and principles for the defense to follow. The danger zones are shown in the figure.

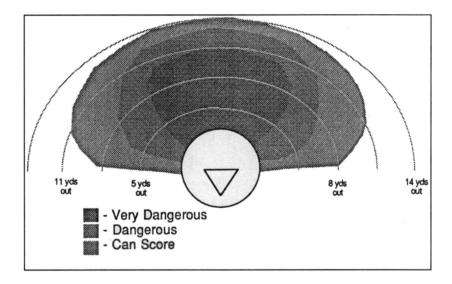

11 yds out   5 yds out   8 yds out   14 yds out

- Very Dangerous
- Dangerous
- Can Score

Team defense lessens the scoring danger

Defensive Principles

Defensive principles vary depending upon what the offense is doing, but, these apply nearly always:

- The man with the ball is the most dangerous player, cover him and don't leave.
- If all defenders are active, involved, alert, aggressive and well positioned the offense has the most difficulty.
- Pressure on the ball, especially stick pressure on the bottom hands eventually produces turnovers
- A shot from a side is less dangerous than one from out front since it narrows the area the keeper protects - shade / drive the player outside toward the goal line
- An unimpeded shot is more accurate than one where the defender's stick pressures the shooter / cutter
- An outside shot that the goalie sees is easier to save than any

inside shot, thus the defense should strive to be compact giving up the outside shot over others.

- A screen makes the shot harder for the keeper to pick up—move defenders and offensive players.
- Slide inside out so that a pass by the ball handler is to a wing, instead of to the crease
- Every slide needs a second slide to cover the most dangerous player left open by the first slide.
- Slide reluctantly since someone is likely left open during the slide.

These principles are discussed further below.

Leader of the Defense

An advanced keeper becomes the leader of the defense. The goalie has an advantage, from a team perspective, in that he faces the ball all the time. He sees the play as it unfolds both offensively and defensively. The keeper can direct the defense accordingly through his talk and actions..

Defensive Preferences

It is better for the defense to give up almost any shot from 11-12 yards or farther out and no shots from 8 yards in. Anyone who shoots from 8 yards or closer should end up knocked down by the defender sliding to the ball. Having your defense understand the dangerous areas leads them to roam less - available to slide and help one another when needed.

It is important for the goalie to know what shots are his / her responsibility and what is the defense's responsibility. If the keeper lets his defense know that he wants then the teamwork improves. For example, if a player, not on the ball, follows his man outside the box, he can't slide to help another. And, if a player playing the ball follows him out so far than when beaten it is hard for the defense to slide, then the that player is too far out. Bringing that player in toward the crease is good goaltending. The coach can't see everything, so the keeper has to help adjust the defense on the field so that the dangerous areas are as protected as circumstances allow.

Adjustments

Adjustments depend on

a) the defense that your are running
b) the personnel involved.

There are various defenses that are used from ZONE to MAN-to-MAN to a number of types of SLIDING defenses (similar to a switching man-to-man in basketball). Every defense has a weakness, just as every offense has a weakness. Part of the offense's challenge is to both find and exploit the weakness of the defense. The goalie probably knows his team's defensive weaknesses from practice. In addition, teams are dynamic things that play weaker or stronger at different times during the game. When the goalie is mature enough, he can adjust the defense to what the offense is doing and/or how the defense is performing. It is up to coaches to teach the keeper the adjustments he/she wants in Zone, Man-to-Man, Man-Down or other defensive schemes in use.

Zone Defense

Zone defenses (where the players play more of an area than a man) are susceptible to teams that cut and feed well and/or overload areas of the field. Few teams use a zone continually since it requires six man coordination, all the time, or the cutters will come open inside and score.

Most teams do not have the talent to play a zone for long. But, it is a very useful defense to stop a dodging team for long enough so that the offense must change what it is doing. Or as a structure for man-down defense.

Man-to-Man Defenses

Man-to-man defenses are good at shutting down a passing / feeding based offense. Pure man-to-man is susceptible to players who can dodge and shoot. Since not all players play defense with the same intensity and effectiveness and not all offensive players are big play players, match-ups in man-to-man are important. The best defenders needs to play the best offensive players.

One goal of an offense is to get a good player on a weaker defender. For example, getting a good attackman to be played by a short stick middie. Offenses will deliberately run picks just to get the defense to switch assignments (to the offense's advantage). The second adjustment is to decide if / when we are going to switch assignment. Usually, if the offensive team has an impact player, the defensive team will dedicate one very good defender to that player. This usually means that that defender does NOT help out other defenders and that almost no one switches assignments to take that offensive player. It takes practice for designated defender to fight through picks and other interference.

Sliding Defense

Many lacrosse teams use a variant of man-to-man defense that involves SLIDES. A slide is a move by one defensive player to another offensive player, usually because that offensive player has gotten by his defender. Team defenses not only slide once but have multiple slides so that the least dangerous offensive player has the least coverage in the process.

The coach, keeper and defense need to agree upon slides and then adjust this agreement or discuss positioning with the defense to make the approach work.

Very much like basketball, the defense can't just show the offense the same set every time. The offense will adjust to the set by running different offensive sets/plays that will break down the defense. There is a further complication in defensive play, when to switch the defensive set and which one to switch to. Usually, this is called by the coaches, but, as we discuss below there are some set changes that goalies may call to adjust to the offense with the guidance from the coach.

Three Man Sliding Defense
The most basic team defense involves having the three close defensemen working together with the goalie. The most basic version of this is the Break 3 fast break defense discussed in Section III. In non-fast break situations the roles are one defender covering the ball, a defender covering the hole (front of the crease) and the off-side defender cheating or shading to the hole. If the defender on the ball is beat, then the crease defender slides to the ball and the off-side defender slides to the crease. If the offense overloads to one side then either the defensemen need to pinch toward the pipes or get sliding help from a middie.

Either slide takes team defense discipline, because the off-side defenders need to play closer to the goal pipes than their man and yet still be able to guard their man should he get the ball.

Getting Back On Track
When total team defense (all six men) is failing, first get the three man defense to work together. A keeper can get his defense together at a time out or after a score and have them reset to first run the three man defense (or get them to pinch more to make it work). Based on this working, then the middies are incorporated. This is not the only defensive alignment that works, but it is fundamental. If the defense is ranging too wide and no slides are being made, then getting into this defense is a start back to better play.

Isolation Defense
Offenses use isolation formations such as the 1-4-1 with the center middie with the ball. With the defense spread in a man-to-man set with everyone covering close, sliding is more difficult. Many teams switch to zone in this situation. The goalie would rather have to make a save on one of the wing shooters with a low angle than try to make a save on a shooting center middie so the zone overloads the middle to make the offense change from what it wants to do. The vulnerability in this defense is a pass followed by an off-side cutter to the ball. Teams use this defense as a change of pace or in special situations as is shown here.

Middie Slides

If the middies are getting beat out front, then there are alternatives; slide from the midfield or slide with a defenseman. If the three man defense is working then a slide from the crease by the inside or crease defenseman is effective. Some offensive teams depend on this slide and feed the crease based on the slide. The two off-side defensemen need to back up the crease defenseman when the ball is at the midfield.

Take 'em Out

You can get help against a great shooter. By making him play out of role or by cutting him off from any passes to him and/or by NOT sliding from the shooter, you can minimize his shooting opportunities. Making others on his team carry the scoring load usually helps your team.

Back SidePicks

At Lake Placid in 1996, we played a team that used a very effective adaptation of an indoor lacrosse play. This play and ones like it involve the attackman on one side of the field carrying the ball toward the midfield while a middie sets a pick at about the goal line extended for the off-side wing attackman. As he comes off this pick the man with the ball feeds him for a shot. This sounds simple, but it is the misdirection of the original attackman that unsettles the defense. If this happens pinch the off-side middie from up top to the crease and pick off the pass. This is another facet of having the defense adjust to the offense.

Attacking Defenses

Most of the above involves more passive techniques. There are attacking defenses. Many teams have one or two offensive players that are not as strong as others. The goal is to isolate that player on one of the better defenders and have him take the ball away. The defense for this is a combined man-to-man and zone with three players playing man-to-man and three playing zone. The men defending the ball, the person to the right of the ball and the person to the left of the ball play them man-to-man and tight. This takes away the closest outlet pass for the man with the ball. The other three play zone with one man in the crease and the other two cutting off passing lanes to the remaining two players. This makes it very difficult to move the ball around the horn and makes the offense change its passing patterns. This rattles the weaker player and the ball will stop with him, where the defender can take it away. This defense is susceptible to good dodging since three players are up close on their men. The back side zone has to be effective, sliding to the dangerous player on dodges.

Another attacking defense funnels a player close to the goal for a big hit. By opening up a lane between the crease and a defender on a wing, an attackman can be lured to drive the post from the rear while the defense is ready to slide from the crease (or far-side) to provide a big hit in the alley between the crease line and the wing defender who turns to hold the driving player in that alley.

When the coach installs one or more of these attacking defenses, the keeper can be taught to both call them and to adjust them to the circumstances.

Man-Down Defense

Man-down defense is the special team of lacrosse. This defense must play with one (or 2 or 3) less defenders than the offensive team due to a penalty on the defensive team. The key to man-down is to give up the longest, lowest angle shots possible. Many teams use a number of zone defenses (2-3, 1-3-1 or 2-3 on a string) depending on what the offense is doing (2-3-1, 1-4-1 or 3-3). There are "rotation" defenses that are used especially against a 2-3-1 offense. Coaches need to teach the keeper the team's various man-down defenses. The advanced keepers will not only better cover the expected shots but will adjust the defense too. Expect the good keepers to lead the defense by his actions, his talk and his adjustments – they will make the D better.

B. In-Goal Techniques

Picking Off Passes

Generally, attempting to pick-off passes, either crossing passes or feeds from the rear, leaves the keeper out of position if the pick-off attempt is missed. Controlling when to try pickoffs is important, so practice them.

Pick-offs on passes from the rear can be accomplished by moving from the center of goal more toward the pipe on the side where the feeder is with keepers hands down a little. On the pass take one step and raise the stick into the path of the ball. This approach leaves passes to the back side of the goal up to the defense to stop and makes it more difficult for feeders to feed inside.

For crossing passes, the best technique is one where the keeper picks it off on the run starting the break. This lowers the amount of hesitation and increases the possibility of a successful result. The keeper needs to be a good stick handler on the move to use this technique.

"Down-the -Line"

A second technique in handling shots by players coming around from behind is taught by Coach Guy Van Arsdale at RIT and is very productive. The technique, called going "Down-the-Line" involves waiting until the last possible moment until it is clear that the shooter is going to go for the long pipe side of the goal and then stepping down the goal line toward the long pipe (away from the shooter) and make the save.

This is very effective since it allows the keeper to get to the ball at the latest possible moment just before it would go in the cage. With good concentration on the ball, this move takes away the tendency of many keepers to be beaten by a bounce shot to the long pipe. Since one steps to the long pipe, the keeper is lower to the ground and can readily pick up the low shot to the long pipe. There are a couple of important points about this technique. First, move down the line LATER than it seem prudent. This negates the shooter faking at the long post and coming back to the near post.

Second, there are times when one must step out to the shooter (especially when the defense is cutting off the shooter's access to the face of the goal). When that occurs, step toward the shot with the short pipe side foot to assure that the near pipe stays covered. Even if the shot seems to be for the long pipe, step with the near pipe foot. This technique assures that the near pipe is covered and lets the keeper step only "Down-the-Line" on shots to the long pipe. He does not have to make a "foot" decision in mid-shot with this technique if he always steps OUT with the near pipe foot and steps DOWN with the far pipe foot when protecting close to the net.

There are two disadvantages to this technique;

1) the footwork is unique
2) stepping away from the shot is counter to the "attack" mode of stepping toward the shot.

For almost all youth and high school goalkeepers, teach the traditional methods until they were very consistent and have the insight in themselves to work with this advanced technique. Then I teach it to them, cooperatively, where they can work it into their repertoire. The technique provides a real edge in close and I heartily endorse it for the more advanced keepers.

Baiting Shooters Some goal keepers actually bait the shooter to shoot at a particular area of the goal. As the shooter goes for this area, the keeper moves to take that area away (hopefully making the save).

Baiting doesn't work, at least not for very long. Other teams will learn to wait for the move and score by shooting where the keeper moved from.

Positioning-for-Strength Keepers do have stronger and weaker areas of their game. For example, if confident on high shots and not confident on low bounce shots, the set up <u>very</u> low (Butt Down). This stance helps get to more bounce shots, somewhat like a baseball shortstop - it is easier to come up from a low stance than to go down from a high one.

Some keepers are less confident off-sides than stick side. For these, set up a little closer to the off-side post inviting the shooter to shoot to that stronger (stick) side.

The difference between baiting the shooter and this positioning is that in baiting the keeper moves deliberately to cover the baited (open) area, while in "positioning-for-strength" the keeper moves with the shot relying on his strengths to make the save. Positioning-for-strength discourages the shooter from shooting into the keeper's weakness, as such, it turns the odds back in the keeper's favor. Baiting can be beaten by the shooter through patience, thus turning the odds in the shooter's favor – avoid baiting.

Keepers need to be continually taught to progress and improve on both their stronger and weaker areas. This means that a positioning-for-strength technique is not an excuse for not practicing to overcome a weakness. Coaches need to help the keeper use positioning techniques to advantage AND help the keeper learn to improve where they are weakest.

C. High Performance Goaltending

In 2006, for the US Lacrosse Coaches Convention, I developed an approach to show keepers where they stood in relation to being the best that they could be. In 2008, the approach was improved for inclusion in this book based on more experience with it. While the section on Evaluating Performance in another chapter shows a keeper's game performance outcomes, this approach is a progress oriented approach.

Getting to Blue   It is called Getting to Blue. The figure and the color one (back cover) show the structure used by the coach and the keeper to agree where the keeper stands in eight categories on a scale from RED (on the bottom of the chart) to BLUE (on the top). The evaluation provides the coach and player insight about what to work on next.

Using the Chart   The next two charts show a college and high school player and where they are in relation to each category. The thick line through each chart shows their current evaluation. Above the line is what to work on. The college player is playing at a higher level and should focus on different improvement areas than the high school player.

← Stronger   Weaker →

Save Range	Save Shots	Save Focus	Save Stance	Save Position	Control	Talk	Clearing
Off Hip Shots Solid	Makes Inside Stuff Saves	Sees ball even in close	Balanced & Ready Early	In Place/ Ready Early	Makes it Easy for Others	Calls Defenses	They Defend His Break
Off Side Low / Bounce Solid	Inside Feed Saves Solid	Watches Ball into Pocket	Leans Into Shot	Hands High on Turns	Helps on Clears	Calls Situations	Throws 40 yards
Stick Side Low/ Bounce Solid	Feeds/Turn Saves Solid	Tracks Ball on Passes	Chest in Front of Hips	Runs/turns into stance on pass/feed	Uses Time for Outlets	Calls Formations	Good Dodger
5 Hole Low/ Bounce Solid	Drive/ Dodge Shots Solid	Watches Ball in Flight w/ hand / eyes	On Balls of Feet	Turns Forward	Controls Ball on Saves	Calls Ball Position	Will Run
Off Side High Solid	Fakes on Shots OK	Watches Ball in A/M Stick	Knees Bent Pigeon Toed	Mirrors Ball Behind	Gets Some Pickoffs	Calls Hot / Two / Slide	Finds / Hits Open Man
Stick Side Hi Corner Solid	High Speed Shots OK	Ball Watching In Glimpses	Top Hand at Eye Level	Adjusts to Ball Position	Runs Out Shots	Clear/ Check Calls	Throws OK 30 Yards
Stick Side Hip to Shoulder OK	Outside Shots OK	Watches Shooter – Ready Early	In Stance Prior to Shot	Dancy Feet	Gets Ground Balls	Self Talk	Throws 20 yards
Only Saves Outside Stick Side Shots		Watches Play - Not Ready	On Heels/ Hands Low	Yields Pipe	Rebounds/ Turnovers	Quiet	Produces Turnovers

Getting to Blue

Grading a Solid College Starter

Save Range	Save Shots	Save Focus	Save Stance	Save Position	Control	Talk	Clearing
Off Hip Shots Solid	Makes Inside Stuff Saves	Sees ball even in close	Balanced & Ready Early	In Place/ Ready Early	Makes it Easy for Others	Calls Defenses	They Defend His Break
Off Side Low / Bounce Solid	Inside Feed Saves Solid	Watches Ball into Pocket	Leans Into Shot	Hands High on Turns	Helps on Clears	Calls Situations	Throws 40 yards
Stick Side Low/ Bounce Solid	Feeds/Turn Saves Solid	Tracks Ball on Passes	Chest in Front of Hips	Runs Into Stance on Pass / Feed	Uses Time for Outlets	Calls Formations	Good Dodger
5 Hole Low/ Bounce Solid	Drive/ Dodge Shots Solid	Watches Ball in Flight w/ hand / eyes	On Balls of Feet	Covers High with Stick	Controls Ball on Saves	Calls Ball Position	Will Run
Off Side High Solid	Fakes on Shots OK	Watches Ball in A/M Stick	Knees Bent Pigeon Toed	Mirrors Ball Behind	Gets Some Pickoffs	Calls Hot / Two Slide	Finds / Hits Open Man
Stick Side Hi Corner Solid	High Speed Shots OK	Ball Watching In Glimpses	Top Hand at Eye Level	Adjusts to Ball Position	Runs Out Shots	Clear/ Check Calls	Throws OK 30 Yards
Stick Side Hip to Shoulder OK	Outside Shots OK	Watches Shooter – Ready Early	In Stance Prior to Shot	Dancy Feet	Gets Ground Balls	Self Talk	Throws 20 yards
Only Saves Outside Stick Side Shots		Watches Play - Not Ready	On Heels/ Hands Low	Yields Pipe	Rebounds/ Turnovers	Quiet	Produces Turnovers

Stronger ↑ / Weaker ↓

Grading a High School Player

Save Range	Save Shots	Save Focus	Save Stance	Save Position	Control	Talk	Clearing
Off Hip Shots Solid	Makes Inside Stuff Saves	Sees ball even in close	Balanced & Ready Early	In Place/ Ready Early	Makes it Easy for Others	Calls Defenses	They Defend His Break
Off Side Low / Bounce Solid	Inside Feed Saves Solid	Watches Ball into Pocket	Leans Into Shot	Hands High on Turns	Helps on Clears	Calls Situations	Throws 40 yards
Stick Side Low/ Bounce Solid	Feeds/Turn Saves Solid	Tracks Ball on Passes	Chest in Front of Hips	Runs/turns into Stance on pass/feed	Uses Time for Outlets	Calls Formations	Good Dodger
5 Hole Low/ Bounce Solid	Drive/ Dodge Shots Solid	Watches Ball in Flight w/ hand / eyes	On Balls of Feet	Covers High with Stick	Controls Ball on Saves	Calls Ball Position	Will Run
Off Side High Solid	Fakes on Shots OK	Watches Ball in A/M Stick	Knees Bent Pigeon Toed	Mirrors Ball Behind	Gets Some Pickoffs	Calls Hot / Two / Slide	Finds / Hits Open Man
Stick Side Hi Corner Solid	High Speed Shots OK	Ball Watching In Glimpses	Top Hand at Eye Level	Adjusts to Ball Position	Runs Out Shots	Clear/ Check Calls	Throws OK 30 Yards
Stick Side Hip to Shoulder OK	Outside Shots OK	Watches Shooter – Ready Early	In Stance Prior to Shot	Dancy Feet	Gets Ground Balls	Self Talk	Throws 20 yards
Only Saves Outside Stick Side Shots		Watches Play - Not Ready	On Heels/ Hands Low	Yields Pipe	Rebounds/ Turnovers	Quiet	Produces Turnovers

Stronger ↑ / Weaker ↓

Keepers aren't the same and with "Getting to Blue" you can adapt workouts to what they need and to areas that the coach and keeper agree upon.

College Player Chart

This player may be well thought of goalie in his league yet there are still key elements of his game to improve including, CHECK and CLEAR calls, using time for OUTLETS, getting into stance on feeds and drives, throwing the ball better and improving save-ability OFF HIP and on FEEDS and ONE-ON-ONEs. These can be incorporated into workouts through situational drills accomplished by the coach, goalie and key players.

High School Player Chart

This player needs to focus on fundamentals. By using off-side situation shooting, drive and feed drills, working on Ball Watching and Early Setup as well as improving stance and setup positioning and footwork, running out shots, and improving talk and throwing, there is a lot to build into daily workouts to help the keeper improve.

Getting to Blue

Each column in the table is covered below. These are summaries of material in previous chapters.

1. SAVE Range

The great shooters shoot corners and the
Great Goalies get there first.

Some high school keepers don't see many of these shooters and thus may have good, even great stats, but haven't faced many accurate corner shooters. In college, especially Division I, the shooters shoot around the keeper's body and shoot for the red. Range is the ability to cover all the corners of the goal smoothly and effectively. The most interesting and difficult range oriented goalie bad habit to overcome is mental. When the goalie thinks that the shot is not make-able or is too wide to attempt the save, he may provide a limited effort to the ball. In many cases, no one has taught him how to make a save that is wider than expected, so these limited moves are overcome-able through better techniques and practice.

Next Step Techniques / Drills

Off Hip Shots Solid	**Over the Top Stick Rotate and Under Stick Rotate Work Sidearm, Overhand, Risers and Fakes**
Off Side Low / Bounce Solid	**On Balls of the Feet or Low will Go – Lots of Reps to Offside – Work Low-Low then Sidearm then Overhand**
Stick Side Low Corner Solid	**Ball Watching Thru Bounce – Drive Low Hand to the Ball Work on Low-Low Shots, then Sidearm then Overhand**
Five Hole Low/ Bounce Solid	**Ball Watching Thru Bounce – Stick Rotate – Chest in Front Work on Low-Low Shots, then Sidearm then Overhand**
Off Side High Solid	**Playing on the Balls of the Feet –Staying Calm Stick Rotation and Off-Side Stepping – Work Off-side Shots**
Stick Side Hi Corner Solid	**Higher Speed Shots – Eyes Glued to Ball – In Good Stance Stepping – Work on Shots with Ball Hidden and Fakes**
Stick Side Hip to Shoulder OK	**Setup and Ball Watching – Work on Stepping and Hand/Stick Drive (Going to the Ball)**
Stick Side Misses	**Medium Speed Reps – Hi to Hi – Work on Stance and Hands**

Improving Save Range – High, Low and Corners

Great range is a product of great save technique;

Hand drive / stick rotation gets the head to the corner faster (with the stick face facing the shot). Gripping the stick tight with the top hand and rotating the bottom hand in front of the top hand forearm on off-side high and off shoulder saves, the stick moves to a more horizontal position dramatically increasing the save range/speed. In all cases, the top hand leads and elbows stay bent to minimize rebounds.

Stepping to the ball gets the hips moving to get the hands to the ball faster and increases the goalie's effective range. Waiting on the ball decreases range and makes the keeper late. Even quick keepers have trouble laying back on the ball, stepping helps in moving all the goalies parts to the ball, increasing effectiveness and range.

Elbows and knees bent (elbows pointing toward the ground) increases reach/speed and minimizes rebounds.

Smooth/Loose   Most goalies will tense up some on high speed shots. Since staying loose (except for the top hand grip on the stick) is vital to range and all saves, overcoming this tenseness is important, especially when there is less time to make the save (close in or high speed). The objective is to be smooth to the ball without any extra motion – being efficient, as Guy Van Arsdale says. To learn this, the keeper needs to see a lot of shots at game speed or faster, first on shots he is good at and then to the next step; corners. When he is saving your high-speed shots, games will seem easy.

Tight Indicators   Learn these indicators and their corrections.

Name	Description	Correction
False Stepping	A reset step with either foot before stepping to the ball	Setup more pigeon-toed, weight on the balls of the feet, not heels, stance wider than shoulder width
Two Moves to Low	Stick rotation and then dropping stick to the ground	Chest in front of the hips and full stick rotation (top hand tomahawk chop to the ball with a wrist twist to keep the stick face toward ball)
Sweep to Low	Both hands sweeping with the bottom hand moving in the same arc as the top (and way outside the hip)	Both elbows pointing down - Tomahawk chop to the ball for stick rotation to vertical – practice 5 hole then stick side and off-side shots with bottom hand drive out toward the shooter and over the ball
Bottom Hand Pull	Gripping the stick with all four fingers of the bottom hand and pulling the stick in or back	Setup with bottom wrist to the back and top two fingers and thumb gripping the stick - Use a toilet paper roll on the shaft for bottom hand grip and teach TOP HAND TIGHT, bottom hand loose
Snap to offside high	Stick rotation to off-side with immediate rotation back during the save yielding many rebounds	Same as above plus show palms to the shooter as the stick head drives up field

High Technique   There is benefit from understanding and applying the most effective save techniques. The stick side high technique involves the simplest moves of driving the top hand using a firm top hand grip to the ball and the bottom hand out from the hip supporting the reach of the top hand AND stepping in a triple step to move the hips to help the hands get to the ball faster. The steps should always be forward to ball side (away from the goal line and out as far as the pipe on the ball side.

Triple Step

The triple step is a short first step with the ball side foot (toes pointed at the shooter and on the balls of the foot) putting all the weight on that foot. The second step pulls the off ball foot up in back of the ball side foot. The third step uses the ball side foot to reset into a wide stance by stepping forward. The keeper steps out of the stance and back in, ready for everything, all on the balls of the feet with knees and elbows bent (to minimize rebounds).

If the 1st step is sideways (meaning toward the sidelines) then the stick is turned by the turn of the body making the keeper less effective. The steps need to be toward the shooter, the chest remains facing the shooter and the elbow remain in front of the chest throughout the save.

Off-Stick High

On the off-stick side high save, the top hand leads to the ball (no change in grip) with the top hand elbow a little below the chin to keep the forearm from blocking the eyes. The bottom hand with wrist to the back of the shaft is driven up in front of the top hand forearm giving full stick rotation and reach to the off-side corner. The triple step starting with the off-stick foot is used to propel the hips ball side to get the hands to the ball quickly (stepping up field toward the shooter).

High Shots

If he is not even consistent on High Shots from 12 yards out then that is where you start until you get him to make those saves consistently and then make those saves from a solid stance with a good triple step to the ball. Focus on high top hand that tracks the ball all the way into the pocket for the keeper to gain confidence on since for the good keeper they should be easy and smooth.

Low Shots

Then move to low shots (LO-LO) and work on stepping, stick rotation and hand and hip drive out toward the ball. Since keepers will be distracted by the bounce and even blink on a bounce shot, it is vital to work on their ball concentration as well as their technique.

Fast Shots

As his confidence grows in this area, go back to Hi-Hi shots that are fast and then fast bounce shots.

Those are the basics. As he/she becomes more accomplished then work on the more advanced techniques involving different shot types/circumstances

2. Save Types

For the higher level goalie, he has got to make all those outside shot saves and all the saves off of drives, feeds, in-close and one-on-one.

Keepers need to practice **all shot situations** to gain the confidence, through repetition in a controlled environment – with feedback from you – that allows him to stay in every shot to the end leading with his top hand to the ball.

Improving Saves by Shot Type and Range

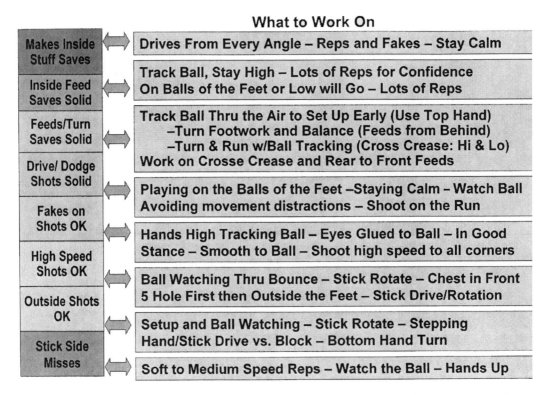

What to Work On

Makes Inside Stuff Saves	⟺	**Drives From Every Angle – Reps and Fakes – Stay Calm**
Inside Feed Saves Solid	⟺	**Track Ball, Stay High – Lots of Reps for Confidence** **On Balls of the Feet or Low will Go – Lots of Reps**
Feeds/Turn Saves Solid	⟺	**Track Ball Thru the Air to Set Up Early (Use Top Hand)** **–Turn Footwork and Balance (Feeds from Behind)** **–Turn & Run w/Ball Tracking (Cross Crease: Hi & Lo)** **Work on Crosse Crease and Rear to Front Feeds**
Drive/ Dodge Shots Solid	⟺	**Playing on the Balls of the Feet –Staying Calm – Watch Ball** **Avoiding movement distractions – Shoot on the Run**
Fakes on Shots OK	⟺	**Hands High Tracking Ball – Eyes Glued to Ball – In Good** **Stance – Smooth to Ball – Shoot high speed to all corners**
High Speed Shots OK	⟺	**Ball Watching Thru Bounce – Stick Rotate – Chest in Front** **5 Hole First then Outside the Feet – Stick Drive/Rotation**
Outside Shots OK	⟺	**Setup and Ball Watching – Stick Rotate – Stepping** **Hand/Stick Drive vs. Block – Bottom Hand Turn**
Stick Side Misses	⟺	**Soft to Medium Speed Reps – Watch the Ball – Hands Up**

Workouts should involve ball movement (feeds from behind and cross crease), player movement (drives), fakes, inside one-on-ones and practicing the techniques (balance, footwork, tracking the ball, …) that help the keeper be ready and distraction free on every shot.

Distractions   Distraction is anything that causes the goalie to not watch the ball. Many times it is caused by the shooter hiding the ball or movement that makes tracking the ball more complicated. Fakes are distraction not just because they misdirect the goalie as to where the ball is going or when it is being shot but because the motion of the fake distracts the goalie from watching the ball. The split dodge with its switch of hands and side the ball is on has the added disadvantage of interrupting the expected body language movements that goalies use as triggers to where the ball is or is going. Thus, the split dodge deserves the most practice repetitions.

Feeds

Similarly, feeds of all types introduce complex pre-shot activities for the goalie including changes in position, footwork to make the change, weight distribution, hand re-positioning and distractions on when/how the ball might be shot. Since the initial position, movement/ footwork, final position and getting settled into the stance is different, each of the sequences needs a lot of practice from both sides of the goal with variations such as drive from the rear right to a middie top left or top right or side right or an attackman crease left. These repetitions provide the goalie with confidence in being in position and ready to make the save under game conditions.

One-on-Ones

Practicing shots in close where the emphasis is on tracking the ball with the top hand while maintaining an aggressive, on-the-balls of the feet stance brings excellent results. But, these drills can be frustrating to the keeper, so keep encouraging him/her that the saves will come and when they do praise him/her a lot re-enforcing the possibility of making that save again.

Drills

Use all the drills to help your keeper progress in Getting to Blue. Focus on the next steps indicated in the evaluation you and your keeper agree are the next steps in his progress to be better. See Chapter 8 Drills, select some and then vary them to help the keeper stay interested/challenged.

3. Save Focus

Watch, Ready, Go and Next

These four things the keeper can control. Focus, especially on making saves, is the critical ingredient to high productivity. Although speed or quickness are very useful, it is almost universal that quick young goalies use their quickness to make up for not being good at watching the ball, for lazy setup/ technique or waiting on instead of attacking the shot. At higher levels of the game this is not enough. All facets of making saves or pickoffs have to be addressed or the keeper leaves a weakness that offensive teams exploit. The hard news is that on most goals the keeper is not at his best – either not ready or not watching.

Watch/Ready

Watch a lot of games and some things become clear;

- Give up 15 goals and your team almost always loses
- Only 5 of these are earned
- On 10 the goalie wasn't ready or was not watching the ball not at his/her best on 10 crucial shots

Working on those 10 where the keeper wasn't at their best produces dividends;

Watching the Ball every second in the offensive box. Use the top hand as guide – watch in 30 second increments, as one would do in a stare down contest. Watching includes in the stick, off the lip, in the air on passes and shots and into the pocket.

Being in a productive ready stance early and continuously means hands up, feet more than shoulder width apart, knees/ elbows bent, wrist to the back of the shaft, weight on the balls of the feet and chest in front of the hips. Ready includes repositioning on passes and drives to be ready again before the shot is released.

Tunnel Vision

It feels like you are looking at the ball through a tunnel or tube. It goes like this. Put your hand up at eye level and to the side of your eye and out in front and look at your thumb. Now rotate your hips and shoulder, turning your body head and hand together while looking at your thumb. Everything past your thumb should blur as you TUNNEL in on looking at your thumb. Then do this with a ball that is thrown up in the air and have the keeper look past his top hand at the ball while tracking the ball with his top hand pointing at the ball wherever it goes – even pointing at the ball in flight. Everything behind the ball should blur and it gets easy to see. Then move to doing that during the Ball Toss drill or lob shots with that top hand guiding vision. This helps in ball focus.

Glimpses

Keepers will fake themselves out – thinking that they are watching the ball but looking at the ball only occasionally. They take a glimpse of the ball then look at the defense, the offense, the shooter or other things. You can see if he is doing this by standing at the top of the box and watch his eyes on scrimmages. If his eyes are not tracking the ball continuously, then they will wander to other things. If you can't stand there, film him. Show him the film, explain full ball watching for 30 seconds at a time (a break will come) and what he is doing. Then encourage him to watch more diligently explaining that he will see the rest of the play in his peripheral vision as he concentrates on the ball (this is a learned effect).

Fast Hands

Using your top hand to track the ball has another advantage. When the top hand is on the side of the line of vision to the ball, the keeper has much faster hand reaction to the ball. Thus, when tracking the ball on a feed in close, not only does that top hand help match the keeper's stick to the receivers stick but puts the keeper in position to move quickly to whatever is done. If the keeper drops his hands on such feeds he is almost always beat unless the shooter hits him. If hands are high and concentration is good on the ball, the advantage goes to the keeper and saves are made – practice this.

Go

This means shifting from ready/watching to attacking the shot by driving the hands and pushing your hips toward the ball to get your hands to the ball faster (waiting on the ball and stabbing or kicking does not)

And, stay in every shot until the end – until it is wide of the goal, until it is in the keepers pocket or until it hits the net behind him. Just throwing his hands and stick to where he thinks the ball will go does not yield high productivity. Watching the ball into the pocket and driving the hands to every shot or pick-off opportunity gets big results. Watching film of Tillman Johnson, Nick Murtha, John Horrigan, Trevor Tierney and Greg Cattrano, one can see that they stay in the shot until the end and that is a lot of why they are so effective.

Next

After this shot prepare mentally and physically (set up and point at the ball) for the next shot. Self talk is at the heart of great focus since the keeper is either getting better or getting worse during the game. Through self-talk the keeper can flush the negative of being scored upon and get set mentally for the next shot by saying what he/she needs to do next to begin going up in performance not continuing the slide down. The strongest of these phrases is, "Get the Next One"

4. Stance

A great stance should make the save easy no matter where or how the ball is shot. Stance makes it easy to rotate the stick to the ball, get to all corners, and step when the keeper goes to the ball for the save.

Stance and being ready are the cheapest part of being good since the stance is accomplished prior to the shot (where all the tension of goaltending really resides). Each technical part of the stance contributes to the concept of "LESS IS MORE."

The less one has to do under the tension of making a save the MORE productive the keeper becomes (in terms of save percentage and big saves under tough conditions). In coaching goalies, many mistakes can be attributed to having to make up with quickness for weaknesses in stance technique. Being a student of stance techniques, simplicity of movement on saves and the principles of going to every shot (hands and steps) cover a wide range of goalie improvement.

Balanced & Ready Early
Leans Into Shot
Chest in Front of Hips
On Balls of Feet
Knees Bent Pigeon Toed
Top Hand at Eye Level
In Stance Prior to Shot
On Heels/ Hands Low

Top Hand at Eye Level – Hands fastest
   – Covers Top of Goal with Stick Face
Both Wrists to the Back of Shaft – Fullest rotation
Top Hand Grip Tight – Accurate stick moves
Elbows Bent/Down – Fastest move down/across
   – Cuts down on rebounds too
Wide Stance – Best corner coverage low
   – Easiest to step to ball side
Knees Bent – Best stepping start
   – Cuts down on rebounds too
Toes Pigeon-Toed – Best push / step to ball
Weight On Balls of Feet – Best mobility / step
Chest in Front of Hips – Best move low
   – Butt out the back, back leaning forward some

A Great Stance Makes Saves Easy

5. Position

Some coaches work more on position than others. Statistically, being ready to make the save is more important than perfect position but three rules of position make the keeper/defense more effective;

1 - Protect the Pipe – The shooter wants to shoot between the keeper and the ball side pipe because there is little defensive help (compared to the middle of the field) against that shot. Shade body/ stance to ball side pipe.

2 - Wide Stance – Especially on the pipe this cuts down the area that the D has to slide in (because the shooter has to come up higher to shoot around the keeper). Wide stance cuts down the defense slide area from 135 square yards to 100 square yards (see the figure) and makes the slide

distance less as a result. Those two effects are defense multipliers (makes the defense more effective). When the feet are wider than shoulder width, it is easier to step to ball side on both sides – making the keeper more effective.

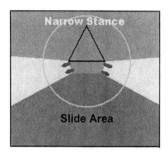 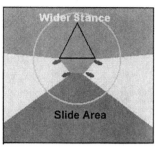

3 - Six Spots – Not 10 or 15 spots to stand. Fewer position spots fosters a stable stance, less dancy feet. If feet are moving too often then the keeper is usually on the wrong foot to push off to step. So get to a spot early to be ready to step.

Associated with this concept of being in your ready stance is getting into the stance early. For passes, feeds and inside rolls/drives, the keeper needs to change position. If he tracks the ball with his top hand AND SETS UP BEHIND HIS HAND, the keeper will be early in his setup and thus in the best position to be ready to make the save. If he is on his heels or hands are down he is not at his best. So, RUN into the stance SETTING UP BEHIND THE TOP hand that is tracking the ball. This movement including the footwork needs to be practiced especially on DRIVE and FEED DRILLS.

6. Control

Control means getting the ball under control after a shot and taking care of it until your offense has it. With the overall goal of the defense to:

**End their Offensive Possession and
Get the Ball to Our Offense**

the keeper can contribute through saves with no rebounds, ground balls, pick-offs, run-outs, no goalie turnovers and great ball handling.

Gaining and keeping control of the ball is vital to effective goaltending. Lacrosse is a game of possessions, any way we can get the ball back without giving up a goal is positive. So, have game goals, for example;

- Saves – 20 (of 30 shots on goal)
- Stuffs – 3
- Ground Balls – 4
- Pickoffs - 1 or 2
- Run-outs – 2
- Making saves on shots that are wide (call them Run-outs if you like) – 2 Set / share these goals with your keeper so he knows how to contribute. If the opponent is a stall oriented team set the goals appropriately.

When working on this with keepers, even in workouts, encourage them to;

- Move to get shots that are as much as a foot wide of the goal, using good technique will not compromise balance and readiness on the on-goal shots.
- Running out every shot that is wide
- Scooping (not raking) any ball on the ground in front of them after a save (making a pass on the run)
- On feed drills work on pick-offs and turns.

Rebounds

Saves are most important but working on saves that don't give up rebounds is also important since many rebounds end up as goals. Rebounds come from a stick too tight, popping the save, locking elbows or knees, not watching the ball all the way into the pocket – ball hits the plastic, or trying to cradle catch the shot – ball hits the plastic. Working on effective stance, grip, stick rotation / hand drive, keeping elbow and knee joints bent throughout, and watching the ball into the stick all stop rebounds.

Rebounds are preventable by stance and save techniques, especially keeping the knees and elbows bent/loose throughout the save. No "give" is required if the elbows are bent, they will absorb the shock of the shot without having to have the hands "give" or go backwards (a bad habit).

Ball Handling

Goalies need to handle the ball well. Work on a wall (stick side and off-stick side) and in ball drills, especially, throwing long and breakout drills. Goalies need to dodge with the ball - put them into dodge and dump drills along with the offense. The goal is zero turnovers on one side and starting the break on the other, so include outlets and ground balls with the shooting in workouts using a 4 second count out load after the CLEAR call so that he is aware of the time he has to get the outlet pass done.

7. Clearing

Clearing is important for a goalie because there is an opportunity to get a fast break in two ways;

- After a save, the keeper can throw the ball out to a teammate while the other team is still charging the goal – Fast Break
- In a set clear D has an extra man to develop into a two on one that continues all the way up the field.

Let the keeper know that he's the EXTRA MAN and needs to be active in the clear until the ball is across the midline.

Breakout Passes The keeper needs to be able to throw an array of breakout passes that are used just as he makes the save or gets a GB and yells CLEAR. The three primary options are:

- Pass to an attackmen at midline – lazy defenses make this available.
- Pass to a middie breaking straight up field – using a lob pass that is long, he can chase it down; never short – gets picked off
- Pass to a banana cut Middie or D-MAN. This is usually a crisp pass with a little lob and long to the outside so the riding A/M can't catch it. If the riding A/M is looking at the breaking M/D-man then throw the outside pass. If the A/M is looking at the goalie have the breaking M/D-man cut in back of the rider and throw the ball there. Practice this read with the goalie and defensive team – it produce fast breaks.

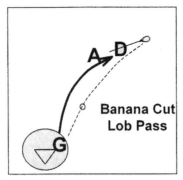

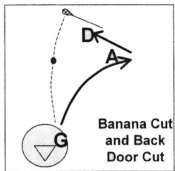

Static Clear

The goalie needs to be involved in the set clear. If the ball is behind the goal he needs to be there so that a pass can be made to him usually on the opposite side of the crease with one foot in the crease while he catches. This stance provides a great target and the opportunity to go back through the crease after the catch.

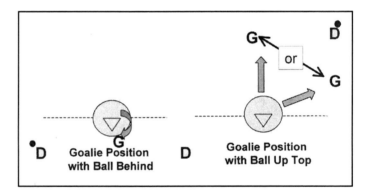

If the ball is above the goal line, the keeper needs to get out from in front of the goal so the team can pass him the ball without mis-throwing it in the goal. Depending on the keeper and the ball handling qualities of the D-men, the keeper is either behind a wing D-man providing an uncovered outlet or is in the middle of the field orchestrating the clear as the team moves up field. In any case, the keeper and his team need to be confident in his ability to catch and throw the ball, even across field, if that is what is open. Practice these situations, positioning and throws every day.

Practice

Control, clearing, banana cuts and cut backs, throwing and other control sequences need to be practiced. This can be done with breakout drills with the goalie and close defense and then incorporate similar sequences as part of full-field practices.

8. Talk

Free Saves

Effective goalie talk produces saves or avoids have to make saves (by the defense keeping the ball off the keeper);

1 - Self Talk – The most important thing you can teach another human being is;

YOU GET WHAT YOU SAY TO YOUR SELF
Said out loud

Teach your keeper to talk to himself between saves to reset him for the next encounter – it is vital. Make sure he talks, not just you, and uses positive affirmations, such as; GET THE NEXT ONE, WATCH THE BALL, HANDS UP, BUTT DOWN, STEP, STEP, STEP. Self-talk is done between shots/saves.

2 - Action Calls – There is only one call that you   have to get during the action and that is CHECK, next is REBOUND, SLIDE and CLEAR all used to tell the defense to change what they are doing and react. Make these calls in warm-ups, 6-on-6, man-up/down and scrimmages as well as games.

3 - Information Calls – These calls help the defense to know how to play and are said calmer than the Action Calls which are shouted. All are very helpful to effective defense (position, who's hot, etc.). But, when the keeper talks and how much is tricky, even for the keeper. If he never talks, then no one, even the keeper, listens. If he jabbers all the time, no one listens. Focus on action calls, then the Break 1,2,3,4,5 calls then position.

4 - Situational Calls – There are sets and action sequences defined by coaches on the defensive half that the keeper needs to know and call (double on sideline inbounds, man-down clear, etc.). For clears these include directing the clear calling for redirect, cross field, etc. passes to make the clear work.

Talk Distraction

Be aware, that watching the defense and making all kinds of information and action calls can take away from watching the ball and therefore is a sophisticated distraction for the keeper. Talking vs. Being Ready and Seeing the Ball is a battle for the keeper so make sure he errs on the watching/ready side. Try to get the calls that are critical but not at the expense of making saves.

Talk to the D

How many of you have seen the goalie and a D-Man arguing after a play. This is usually because the goalie was embarrassed on a shot that was in close because the D-MAN didn't keep the shooter out. Help your keeper understand that when defensive play breaks down it is HIS TURN to step up. Since the game is one of possessions, the keeper should cheer for every defensive ground ball, pickoff, good clear, push out, check or run-out and then that defense will play for him and allow him some slack should a shot go in the keeper should have had. If the keeper talks up the defense, they will play for him/her.

Defensive Calls
As the keeper learns the defenses, he should call them out to the team. For example, when the offense is in a circle (no inside O players), it is likely that near-man adjacent help is provided. For some teams this is called Near Man and should be shouted out by the goalie as the offensive sets up that way. Similarly, when the circle offense cuts into a 1-3-2, 2-2-2, 1-4-1 or 2-1-3 formation, the defense formation/slide package changes. The keeper needs to see this change and call the defense to use, such as the Princeton Tiger slide defense many teams call Tiger or a zone or whatever other schemes the defensive coaches use .

Ready Battle
Talking and being ready are at odds with each other. Most keepers will not talk at all until they become more confident. And, talking can take away from the keeper being ready and/or moving to the shot to make the save. As in-goal save confidence and ability improves then slowly demand more of the keeper on talking. Then talk with consistent saving will multiply the defense's effectiveness overall.

9. Corrections

Corrections are techniques to help improve the keeper. Basic corrections involve stance, watching the ball, going to the shot and getting ready for the next one. Some more advanced issues are covered in the table below:

Save Performance Corrections		
Name	**Description**	**Best Fix**
Late on shots	Hands not moving with the ball and late to the shot – possibly not ready or watching shooter instead of ball	Work on top hand tracking, good stance and aggressive move to the shot Six Yard Drill makes the keeper watch the ball or get beat

Save Performance Corrections

Name	Description	Best Fix
Late Inside	Keeper gets beat on inside shots – probably pulls hands in, leans back into block mode	Teach that saves can be made inside by keeping hands up and pointing at the ball in the stick – always too soon to try to block a shot with body, block mode
	Not watching the ball	Six Yard Drill and Six Yard Drill w/fakes, Ball Toss Drill
Rock 'n Kick	Keeper steps only with ball side foot and late due to rocking back on the off-side foot during the shot	Get weight off the heels by turning toes toward shooter – get keeper doing triple step every time
Late up high	Goalie is beat in the high corners – probably seeing the ball late	Hands up to track the ball – teach watching the ball in the stick and off the lip - Six Yard Drill
	Goalie beet to high corners – probably rotating stick during save	Shift grip emphasis to top hand with no shaft spin - Make sure that hands are one forearm length apart
Bouncers going in	Bouncers outside the feet go in consistently – probably pulling bottom hand in thus pulling the stick head away from either low corner	Teach punching the top hand over the ball and a full stick rotation to vertical (top hand tomahawk chop w/wrist twist) – get stepping
Shots off feeds going in	Drops hands and/or leans back as the feed reaches the shooter	Teach tracking the ball with the top hand and pushing the hands away from the chest on the turn/reposition to stay on balls of the feet Feed Drills
Good Warmup Bad Game	Seems to be late on getting to a lot of shots	Change warm-up to include fakes, feeds and drives for game-like condition Six yard drills w/fakes

Save Performance Corrections		
Name	**Description**	**Best Fix**
Lots of Rebounds	Snap to Off-Side w/ ball coming out after initial save	Bend knees and elbows with wrists to the back, hold the top hand grip tight, bottom hand loose with full rotation
	Ball pops up and out on high saves	Keep elbows bent throughout the save and stop dropping hands/punching the stick up
	Ball pops out	Loosen top hand bottom fingers so that wrist motion is available to absorb shot momentum - Keep elbows and knees bent throughout saves – Get stick restrung with less tension pocket
Bad Outlets	Keeper can't throw long or is inconsistent throwing accurately	Teach the keeper to turn trunk, hips and toes to point to the sideline (shoulder tips in line with the target and throw overhand, not sidearm Tighten a stick with a big bag

D. Alternate Techniques

Over the years of research, discussion, testing and validation of goalie techniques, drills, methods and factors, there have surfaced some differences of opinion between coaches. Until 2008, this book covered what I considered the best of these, but, there are some other considerations. First, there are multiple effective techniques in some areas. Second, the game needs goalies and goalie coaches. So, judging these differences as right or wrong and/or branding their proponents as bad or good coaches is inappropriate. This chapter talks about these differences in part to honor those coaches who take on the difficult task of coaching keepers and in part to indicate the strengths and/or weaknesses of each.

Areas

The areas covered (with my preferences underlined) are;

- Top hand at eye height vs. top hand shoulder height
- Splayed feet vs. pigeon toed stance
- Shoulder width vs. wider than shoulder width stance
- Top hand tight grip vs. bottom hand tight grip
- Hands first vs. feet first move on saves
- Cradle catch low vs. low trap saves
- Mirror vs. same side setup on ball behind
- Through net or around the corner ball tracking behind

- Off side shot hand sweep vs. propeller rotate save
- High arc vs. low arc position on shots

Hand Height

Traditional goaltenders have had their top hand at shoulder height. The idea here is that the top hand / stick is about equal distance from all corners in this stance. There are good goalies with their top hands at shoulder height that have learned quickness to all corners.

More recently there is awareness that there is natural higher hand speed if the hand is to the side of the line of vision to the ball. Boxers use this high hand speed to counter-punch and soccer keepers use it to not only move quickly to the ball but to use the learned action that the body will follow the lead of the hands. Using this technique coupled with a tomahawk chop of the top hand to low saves (making that move fast via the leverage of a propeller motion) also allows the keeper to cover more of the top of the net – very useful on shots close in – while still having quick coverage to low corners.

Further, tracking the ball with the top hand improves concentration and reaction giving the goalie an edge on feeds and fakes.

Foot Position

Traditional goalie instruction has set the feet shoulder width apart to provide the keeper a good foundation where the keeper can maintain his stance for extended periods. This usually means feet splayed (toes pointed outward) and weight back mostly on the heel of the foot.

This position although comfortable can make stepping to the ball difficult since at some point stepping (more than one step/ kick) is predicated upon getting weight on the balls of the feet and positioning the back foot to point toward the destination so it can push the body as the front foot steps toward the shot (especially for multiple step moves). Having the feet pointed at the shooter or a little pigeon-toed facilitates back foot push.

Similarly, a wider than shoulder width stance speeds the 1st step (and aids on covering more goal longer, especially when a player comes around). In a shoulder width stance, stepping involves shifting some weight to the off-ball foot prior to pushing. In the wider than shoulder width stance, the feet are mildly braced to the middle and a lift of the ball side foot immediately starts the body in the direction. The combination of a little pigeon-toed aids in the back foot pushing the body toward the ball. Additionally, the wider stance provides more range to low shots even without stepping.

But, we have seen effective goalies with different foot positioning, so there is more than one stance that works.

Dominant Hand   Some keepers grip the stick tightly with the bottom hand and loosely with the top. With this grip there are tendencies during the save to rotate the stick in the top hand or pull in with the bottom hand. Both decrease either the area of the pocket facing the shot or the range to corner shots. Further, a four-finger grip with either hand restricts the amount of propeller rotation available yielding interesting techniques for off side saves. Many of these interesting techniques are slower than propeller alternatives.

The grip for a goalie stick, both hands should involve the top two fingers and thumb so that full propeller rotation is available. With the top hand grip tight and no changes in grip during the save, the stick goes where the top hand takes it while maintaining maximum stick face toward the ball. The top hand grip should be so strong that the head will not turn in the hand when hit. The bottom hand needs to be very loose to avoid pulling in with it during the save and to provide the most effective pivot for propeller saves to all corners.

1st Move   Occasionally, one will see a goalie that is taught to step first to the shot with the hands following. This seems to be correlated to coaches and goalies whose emphasis is blocking the shot. Goalies with feet first approach also seem to pull their hands into their chest on saves. This limits the area that can be covered because the hands are not free to rotate the stick to the ball quickly. But, there have been at least two All-American goalies that step first. Isn't it interesting how adaptable humans are?

The hands first emphasis is consistent with making the saves with the stick pocket using the body as a backup to a miss with the hands. Since it is critical to move the body (via stepping) to move the hands to all areas and to the ball quickly, the best of all worlds is move hands and feet simultaneously. Even at that, the hands need to lead since they provide the most adjustment to the ball

Low Saves   Some goalies use a two handed cradle catch of shots, even low ones, with a move that has both hands rolling the wrists (top hand in toward the forearm and bottom hand rolling away). The advantage is that this minimizes rebounds and therefore maximizes the chance to start the break immediately after the save.

There are two disadvantages; the stick face is turning (diminishing the area in front of the ball) at a critical time and it is very difficult to get to certain areas of the goal (off-side elbow, shoulder and low corner) using this technique. Those who use this effectively (Rullman, Sothoron, Schmolie) have strong hands, excellent timing and extraordinary footwork. So, this can be effective.

The alternative is the low trap save where the keeper uses a propeller motion to the low area to cover with the top hand driving the stick head to the ball (tomahawk chop) and the bottom hand driving out over top of the ball(so that the stick handle is farther up field than the head). This causes the ball to hit the pocket and stop. It is then picked up to start the break. The disadvantage is loss of immediate control of the ball. The advantage is that the propeller motion allows for the same fast save technique to work to all corners and side of the goal.

Ball Behind Feeds

Some keepers look around the corner (around the pipe) at the ball when it is behind the goal while remaining set up with the chest, hips and feet facing up field. The idea is that when the ball is fed in front or the player drives to the front the keeper is already in position. That is correct.

The alternative is to face the ball behind and turn with an efficient pivot when the ball is fed or the player drives across the goal line extended. If the keeper turns on the balls of the feet and points at the feed (or into the driving player's stick) with his top hand, then the keeper is ready and concentrating on the ball – two big keys to success.

Cross Crease Feeds

When the ball is thrown cross crease, some keepers are taught to pivot back into the goal and then move from in the goal to a ready position just outside the far pipe. The disadvantage is that any step backwards is slower than a forward move and a step backward technique may resurface at some other critical time. For that reason, one simple rule is never step backward in goal play; step forward, pivot forward, etc.

The alternative is to pivot on the pipe foot and run to the opposite pipe while continuing to point at the ball with the top hand. This can get the goalie into the ready stance at the far pipe sooner making for more save possibilities

But, it is the tracking of the ball while moving that is the productive part and the footwork is secondary.

Off-side Save

Some goalies are taught on the off side save (hi or lo) to pull their hands to the side of the chest changing the grip on both hands to keep the stick face facing the ball. The high move is different than the low move where, on the low move, the bottom hand is pulled up to the off side shoulder and the top hand is pushed to the off-side hip. This technique has two vulnerabilities; there is a tendency low to lift the stick yields goals on shots that bounce under the stick and there is little effective movement for off side elbow and shoulder shots.

Using the rotate/propeller approach, keeping the wrists to the back of the shaft and elbows pointing downward, saves can be made over the top for shots from the top corner down to the top of the knee by pushing the bottom hand in front of the top hand forearm. This is fast and provides excellent range. For low the same grip yields a propeller motion with the top hand going under the bottom hand to cover the low corner. This takes practice, but seems to yield more off-side saves once learned.

Arc

There is lots of discussion of arc. Low arc, close to the goal line, provides the most reaction time (farther from the shooter) and the shortest route to the far pipe on cross-crease feeds. It is the dominant arc for men. If the keeper's butt is in the goal, the shooter can and will shoot it off the thigh into the net, so, be far enough out that that can't occur.

High arc, closer to the crease line, gives up reaction time while cutting off the shooters angles (sees less net) and makes the route to the far pipe longer. It is the dominant arc for women. If the shooter shoots high bounce shots from way outside (>12 yards), the high arc assures that the bounce over the shoulder goes over the goal.

The most effective arc is a combination. Use a high arc for shooters that are far outside (foils outside high bouncers) and who are very close to the crease (cuts down angles). User low arc against passing teams - re-setup is effective and quick. And, arc and position are not as important as ball-watching (not shooter watching) and being ready prior to the shot.

Coaches

It is easy to say that one or more of the above techniques is right or wrong. Or more important that a goalie coach who teaches or doesn't teach one of these is good or bad. All the goalie coaches that I know have differences. And all the goalie coaches who take the time to teach goalies are to be commended because their efforts are critical to advancement of the game and to helping prospective keepers that otherwise might not progress.

And, of course, not all keepers are the same so there is room for diversity in players and techniques. That is why I attend as many goalie clinics as I can to learn additional techniques and methods of teaching this unique position. I hope you will do the same.

CHAPTER 10

Goalkeeping Summary

Throughout this book, there are a number of key principles and proven suggestions that make goal tenders and goal tending coaches better. If the player is willing, has the courage to learn until he become adept, has some athletic ability (i.e. quickness and coordination) and concentrates on goaltending, then he or she can become a good goaltender. As a coach, when I go to clinics, I am looking for the clinic notes that I can review and apply. This chapter is those notes.

Overall

Break down instruction into parts:

Focus - This means always Seeing-the-Ball and being Ready for the Shot

Ready/Position - This means making the shooter make a great shot, around the keeper.

Help the Defense - This means Talking, calling out ball position and slides.

Reaction - This is Making-the-Save by use of good stance, good hand position and hand drive, strong step to the shot, stick rotation to the ball and soft hands to avoid rebounds.

Run the Break - This is corralling-the-ball, finding the right player to pass to, making the pass and watching our team score.

Attitude - Managing the goal disappointment es into preparation for the next save.

Concentration

Lapses in concentration cause most goals, focus is key;

1 - **Concentrate to see the seam in the ball -- watch the ball -- it's critical**

2 - Constantly adjusting position helps to stay in the game

3 - Take a step, it helps attitude (attack) and concentration

4 - Set up early, it makes the save easier

5 - Hands up, looking-over-the-thumb are keys to concentration

6 - Get in shape ("Fatigue makes cowards of us all"), it helps in keeping the hands up and the legs bent

7 - Use down field "Markers" to aid in resetting position

8 - Bounce, Scream, Clang your helmet -- they all help keep the keeper "UP"

9 - Play for 30 seconds at a time, a break will occur where the keeper can relax and gather himself

10 - Talk to the defense -- it keeps you in the game

Position DOs   Being in the right place is vital in goal keeping -- it allows good technique to be applied and it makes the shooter work to score;

1 - Be one step way from making the save.

2 - Face the ball, ALL THE TIME and watch the ball, even in flight. (it is the key to flowing to the shot)

3 - When the ball is behind, face the ball handler, then on feeds or shots, take one step to the post and one to the shooter.

4 - Force the perfect shot by covering the other areas (the near pipe especially

5 - Play the shooter's hands -- low hands means get low, you can always come back up with the shot

Position DON'Ts   There are position don'ts;

1 - Don't move out of the crease to hit the offensive player unless there is time to recover to stop the rebound

2 - Don't try to pick off crossing passes, the offense will use a fake pass to move the keeper and then score with him out of position

Talking   Talking to/with the defense is a form of "free save". When they are coordinated and active, they will make take-aways and block shots that would otherwise end up with shots on goal;

1 - Call out the ball position, LOUDLY (i.e. "Ball Left Front", "Ball Right Pipe")

2 - Call out all feeds with a "**CHECK**",

3 - Call for help with a "**HOLD**" or "**SHOOTER**" when a shooter is in shooting position or "**BINGO**" when a slide is needed

4 - Call out all shots, "**SHOT !!**", many defenders will step into the shot.

5 - Call for defense slides with a loud "**SLIDE**"

6 - SPRINT after every shot that misses -- this is another form of "free save" since every time the keeper is closest to the ball when a shot goes out of bounds, the keeper's team gets the ball. This hustle gets a lot of defense respect.

Fast Breaks   Many teams live to fast break. It is their most potent offense (since it means having an extra offensive man against a sliding defense). It is very important to have a solid fast break defense with an ACTIVE GOAL TENDER;

1 - The keeper calls out that a fast break is coming; "**FAST BREAK!!**"

2 - As the point man slides and the ball is passed, the keeper calls out for the whole unit to slide, "**SLIDE**"

3 - The keeper plays the best position, moving quickly with the passes, to make the offense make a "perfect shot" (instead of them shooting at a nearly empty net).

Stance-DOs   Stance is the part of setup that makes saves easier, more
consistent and smoother.
1 - Play ready but "loose"
2 - Take a step to the shot every shot
3 - Bent joints mean good range
4 - Feet that are a little pigeoned-toed saves time to the ball
5 - Hand grip is key to stick rotation
6 - Hands up, "looking eye-thumb-ball" brings the body into play
7 - Lead foot forward, stops interference with the other knee and
    provides better attacking balance
8 - Butt down means better range
9 - Bottom hand forward of the top hand, tilt the stick head back
    slightly means better stick rotation to the ball.

Stance - DON'Ts   There are techniques that hurt goalie play, such as,
1 - Locked knees means higher goals allowed
2 - Hands down means being late on shots
3 - Slew footed stance means two steps to the save (the keeper will be
    late to the ball).
4 - Elbows high means the grip is restricting stick rotation movement

Saves - DOs   Keys to consistent saves;
1 - Play ready but "loose" with a strong top hand grip.
2 - Use a good stance, set up shading to your weakness just a bit (i.e.
    low or off-side)
3 - Drive hands and take a step to the shot every shot
4 - Use a propeller motion of the stick for all saves except stick side
    high.
5 - Keep the elbows in front of the chest on all saves
6 - Let the whole face of the stick stop the shot, then corral it in
    front of the chest.
7 - Face the ball all the time, concentrating on the ball,
8 - With the ball behind, step to the pipe then to the shooter.
9 - Play for 30 seconds at a time, concentrating, as the leader of the
    defense
10 - Talk with the defense and they willl play better even blocking
    some shots and prevent others.
11 – Focus on Watch, Ready, Go and Next to stay on top

Save - DON'Ts   There are techniques that hurt goalie play, such as,
1 - Don't set up with hands down (it means loading -up to move)
2 - Don't play too far from the near pipe
3 - Don't bait it rarely works for long
4 - Don't get down on yourself so the last shot affects the next save
5 - Don't watch the man, the motion, defense or shooter's eyes
6 - Don't let up after the first move, save or shot

7 - Don't stab at the ball, it means misses

8 - Don't try to catch each shot, it means that the stick face is sometimes out of position

9 – Don't be too impatient to progess, it will come.

Throwing

The overall keys to good throwing are;

1 - Practice throwing a lot, long accurate throws.

2 - Turn the feet and body to the side--the throwing stance if very different from the saving stance.

3 - Rock back on the back foot with the stick near horizontal, drive the hands forward and pull down with the bottom hand.

4 - Finish with the bottom hand nearly hitting the top hand's elbow.

Throwing where the hands go across the chest (with a big shoulder turn) produces erratic throws.

Catching

Catching is different from saves;

1 - Practice catching a lot, it makes for good ball handling.

2 - Like throwing, turn the body to one side and present a high target (just above the head).

3 - Give with the hands as ball strikes the pocket and then cradle.

Clears

Clears are part of the team OFFENSE. A well executed clear results on a 2 on 1 or an extra man break on goal. A broken clear results in shots on your keeper.

1 - Take three looks (left point, center, right point) to throw a outlet pass from the crease before exiting to the rear.

2 - Have one defender on one side of the goal as the keeper's outlet if no up field pass is available.

3 - Have the keeper be active (or the man advantage is lost)

4 - Use a three across clear that spreads the defense and makes it easier to get the ball up field in the required 10 seconds (boys).

5 - Swing the ball from one side of the field to the other, this creates a two-on-one advantage.

6 - Have an attack pick play available for the keeper should he carry the ball across the mid-line.

Drills

Drills provide needed repetitions for the keeper.

1 - Practice on your own, team practice is not enough

2 - Catch and throw a lot, it helps to become a better ball handler.

3 - Walk-the-Line drill improves technique through save simulation

4 - Drill, drive and similar drills mirror game situations, use them.

Conditioning

Fatigue is the enemy of a keeper;

1 - Get in shape and stay in shape – 100 stick jump overs per day

2 - Concentrate on quadriceps (upper legs) and deltoids (top of

shoulders) – 100 deep squats and 100 military presses 3-4 times a week

3 - Stretch out all the muscles used in goal keeping (gluts, calves, achilles, quads, hamstrings, upper back)

4 - Run wind sprints UP HILL (with your stick raised)

Warm-ups

Warm-ups are the coaches chance to work with his keepers;

1 - Work through the three stages (seeing, reacting, attacking) giving the keeper a chance to "warm up"

2 - Work each quadrant of the goal (upper left, upper right, lower left, lower right) while walking in a arc 11-13 yards from goal.

3 - Move to "worm burners" at high speed to work in low shots.

4 - Move to overhand bouncers at high speed

5 - Have a behind attackman feed to out front shooters

6 - Challenge the goalie to a "best of 10" shots -- this shows him that he is capable of stopping shots. It is important to shoot hard, keepers know if your are holding up.

7 - Make warm up adjustments (minor reminders) before games, more instruction can be done at practice.

8 - Give the keepers as many repetitions as they can stand, they will improve with practice.

Coaching

Goalkeeping is a lonely position, building a relationship with the keeper is vital to having him / her progress;

1 - "People (keepers) need to know that you care before they care what you know"

2 - Be careful when and what you change in a goalie's style or technique, adjusting slowing is better.

3 - A coach needs to with the goalie regularly, scrimmages (or warm-ups by other players) provide only limited help to a goalie's improvement

4 - Adjustment 1 - Teach the keeper a basic to return to (esp. "Watch the ball")

5 - Adjustment 2 - Talk with the keeper (almost constantly)

6 - Adjustment 3 - "Go Nuts" on good plays.

7 - Adjustment 4 - Give ONE adjustment to the keeper at a time.

8 - Adjustment 5 - Get ready for the NEXT SHOT

9 - Count fast break starts, stuffs, and misses to evaluate performance.

10- Get the goalie to talk with you about instruction/ adjustments (i.e. Does that make sense?, Can you do that ?)

11- Teach the keeper to learn from each shot and adjust himself.

12- Sandwich your criticism, it goes down easier.

13 - Consider holding your sideline comments until you can speak to the keeper one-on-one, their job is embarrassing enough, being further criticized publicly by the coach goes down hard.

14 - Challenging the keeper to do better works -chiding doesn't.

Attitude   Successful coaches teach successful, IMPACT goalkeepers to learn
                      to:
                      1 - Attach the shot
                      2 - Direct the defense
                      3 - Aggressively play the ball/pass
                      4 - Actively clear the ball/start fast breaks
                      5 - Talk to the defense constantly
                      6 - Make the save
                      7 - Inspire the team by their winning / combative attitudes
                      8 - Believe that they can make the save, every time
                      9 - Recover quickly to make the next play when they don't
                      10 - Treat their defense well, they play better for him

Summary   Goalkeeping is a wonderful and initially frightening place to play
                      lacrosse. The position can be taught. I hope that these notes help
                      coaches teach their tenders to be successful.

INDEX

Weston Lacrosse
www.thegoalieman.com
301-294-3234
cell: 443-418-5613
westonlax@aol.com

ABOUT THE AUTHOR

"Coach Weston has a passion for the game of lacrosse that one cannot measure," says Towson University head coach Tony Seaman. "His ability to work with goalies, develop their skills and detail their weaknesses is unparalleled." Recipients of Jon's tutelage include Johns Hopkins' Brian Carcaterra who was a first team All-American in 1998, Towson's John Horrigan, an honorable mention All-American who led the Tigers to the NCAA Final Four in 2001, Towson's Reed Sothoron, an honorable mention All-American and many youth and high school keepers nationwide.

Jon began his lacrosse career as a midfielder in 1965, initially playing intramurals at Johns Hopkins, for the Carling Lacrosse Club (1968) and then the Bowie Lacrosse Club (1969-75) in the United States Club Lacrosse Association (USCLA). After coaching for the first years of the Central Atlantic Lacrosse League (now the All American Lacrosse League) he retired briefly, returning to club ball over 20 years ago as a practice/backup goalkeeping novice. In 1998, he represented the United States in goal at the World Games in the inaugural championships for Grand Masters (over 45 years old) teams.

He continues to coach and play goal (mostly), defense and attack on grand masters and half century (over 50) teams in Vail, Lake Placid, Charm City (Baltimore), the Florida Lacrosse Classic and Ocean City Tournaments.

He helped found the Magruder High School lacrosse club in 1989 as the head coach. He was a member of Coach Seaman's Towson Tiger staff from 1999-2002 and again in 2004, coaching the goalies. 2003 he was an assistant coach at Oakton High School, Virginia State Champs, and coached goalies for the American University women's lacrosse team. 2006 he was back at American and now coaches the defense and goalies at Oakton.

He authored a book entitled "Lacrosse Goaltending for Coaches (Players Too)" and has been featured in lacrosse periodicals. He continues to lecture and demonstrate at clinics around the country. Another book is in the works too; "Lacrosse Strategy" or "Why we don't call plays". Look for it in the near future.

CPSIA information can be obtained at www.ICGtesting.com
Printed in the USA
BVOW060950060313

314859BV00005B/90/P